A CRIMINAL JUSTICE HANDBOOK

THE HIDDEN TRUTHS WITHIN OUR LEGAL SYSTEM

J.B. Simms

Erik Publishing

Names: Simms, J. B. (James B.), author.

Title: A criminal justice handbook: the hidden truths within our legal system / JB Simms.

Description: St. Petersburg, FL: Erik Publishing, 2019. | Previously published in 2017 as Incest within the criminal justice family. | Includes bibliographical references.

Identifiers: ISBN 978-0-578-55175-3 (ebook) 978-0-578-69255-5 (print)

Subjects: LCSH: Criminal justice, Administration of--United States. | Criminal justice, Administration of--United States--Corrupt practices. | Justice, Administration of--United States. | Criminal law--United States. | Police corruption--United States. | Criminal procedure--United States. | BISAC: LAW / Criminal Law / General. | LAW / Criminal Procedure. | POLITICAL SCIENCE / Law Enforcement.

Classification: LCC HV9950 .S56 2019 (print) | LCC HV9950 .S56 2019 (ebook) | DDC 345.73--dc23.

Don't miss other books written by J.B. Simms

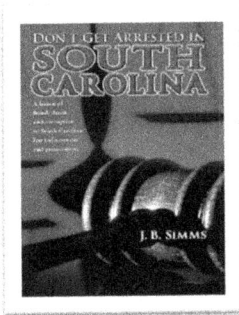

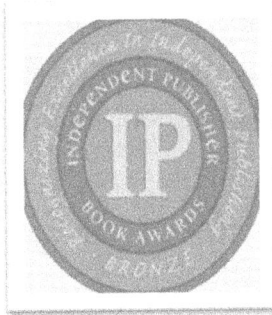

Don't Get Arrested in South Carolina

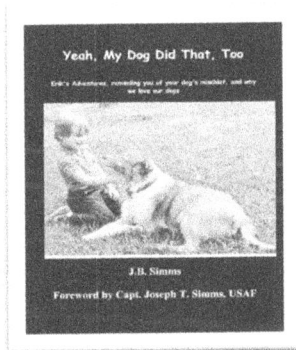

Yeah, My Dog Did That, Too

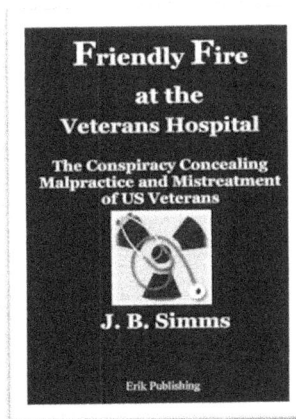

Friendly Fire at the Veterans Hospital

Contents

Dedication

This book is being dedicated to my son, Joe, his daughter, Olivia, and my daughter Megan Ravenscroft. My wish is they learn the lessons within this book to be aware of not only the system, but of human nature involved in decisions made by persons having power over another.

Acknowledgements

The first two persons I thanked for their work on the first edition were my friend, C.J. Tinder, and my son, Maj. Joseph T. Simms (who was a Captain at the time of publication). Ms. Tinder has always been very valuable friend and will correct me when needed. My son, Joe, made suggestions with respect to structure which was very helpful.

Alexandra Camazine, of Newport Beach, CA was instrumental in consulting with formatting and editing the first edition and her insight was valuable to me.

This second version involved a title change, cover change, and edits. Joe Simms, C.J. Tinder, my long-time friend Hite Miller, and Dianne Helm (Helm Publishing) endured constant emails to see my changes to the cover, and to them I owe a debt of gratitude. Ms. Tinder has the keen eye to see a flaw I would not see. Their confidence was motivating.

Dianne Helm was consulted almost daily in the publishing of this second edition, and I am very grateful for her input. If any of you have wrestled with an editor, you know the anxiety; submitting the "final draft" and getting the response that something "was found.". Diane gets special thanks.

Preface

Our criminal justice system is not broken. Our criminal justice system works; the way it works is unknown to most citizens as well as persons who are arrested, who might then become defendants. Within this book you will learn that the people who work in the criminal justice system act as a family with secrets, and the secrets tell you how the system really works.

The three main elements of the criminal justice system are crime, profit, and secrets. People involve themselves in this arena because they make the decision to join and participate. Crime pays, and all the family members benefit. The "pay" is either monetary, career advancement, or power. This handbook details the responsibilities and relationships of each family member. Secret collaboration between a prosecutor and law enforcement, prior to an arrest, can result in targeting a person as a vendetta, effectively causing damage to a reputation even if the arrested person has charges dropped or is found not guilty. The other three family members come into play after the warrant is issued, and the game begins.

Each member of the criminal justice system has their own agenda or motivation: personal, professional, financial, money, job security, power, ego, sex, political position, access to criminal enterprise, adrenaline, contribute, to society, an outlet for aggression, or the thrill of the hunt.

1)   Prosecutor- to obtain a conviction, but not necessarily pursue the truth, get re-elected, keep their job, use the job for validation in private practice.

2)   Defense Attorney- to get a deal his client will accept, be a friend with the prosecutor, and more importantly, to get paid.

3)   Defendant- to get out of jail, and back to the life as he/she knows it.

4)   Law Enforcement- to arrest the person named on the warrant, be validated by the prosecutor, and not be caught being corrupt.

5)   Bail Bondsman- to ensure the defendant/suspect always goes to court, get repeat business from defendants/suspects, and catch every fugitive.

It works the way the five family members in power want it to work, and the most powerful person in the group is the prosecutor.

Many books have been written about prosecutors and the legal system; most being law professors, constitutional scholars, and a few defense attorneys. The reason practicing defense attorneys do not make much of an issue about the corruption in the system is because of their relationship with all the other family members of the system. There are favors to go around for everyone.

My perspective is that of a former private investigator and bail bondsman. I was a private investigator, for over 25 years, and a licensed bail bondsman from 2004-2006. I conducted five undercover operations from 1981-1983. My first murder case defense trial began in January 1986 on the day the space shuttle exploded. In 2004, a bail bond company became my client. I found missing persons for them, as was my talent.

One day they asked me to assist in the apprehension of a fugitive. I was 50 years old and thought I was too old to be wrestling fugitives.

I continued for 18 months as a licensed bail bondsman. I assisted in getting innocent people released from jail as a PI and testified in court. I also have apprehended fugitives as a bondsman, arresting them in some scary situations. I do not lean to either side of any argument; you are either honest or you are an idiot by trying to make me think you are honest.

I have been in the battle with all the elements of the system, assisting and fighting against all parties. My book, Don't Get Arrested in South Carolina, detailed an account of a wrongful arrest and a two-and-a-half-year journey with the defendant and me as the private investigator. Four defense attorneys betrayed the defendant, all wanting either a statement implicating someone else, or the defendant taking a plea. The defendant did neither, and I became the person defending the defendant against the prosecutor, and those in the prosecutor's office. I will refer to this story from time to time.

This book is not about law enforcement responding to a call. Much attention has been given to the presence of law enforcement in localities, stating that law enforcement is overbearing. I totally disagree. If someone throws a brick at a cop, injures a cop, and destroys private and public property, that person needs to be arrested. I admire the cops who go into harm's way, and those who save lives, but corruption is reality.

This handbook exposes the corruption which occurs before and after the arrest, before and during court proceedings, as well as corruption during information gathering.

As you watch crime stories on television and in movies, you see good guys and bad guys along with the stereotypes.

The usual stereotypes are (1) hard-nosed morally pure underpaid prosecutors trying to put a defendant into prison (2) law enforcement risking their lives to catch criminals (3) defense attorneys battling law enforcement and prosecutors (4) immoral defendants, and (5) the opportunistic bail bondsman.

There is a bit of truth to each stereotype, and a bit of creative license in the portrayal of each element of the criminal justice system. Each is a member of the criminal justice family and know how to play the game.

Within this handbook, I will be using the word "defendant" to describe the arrested person. The arrested person is a suspect until the arrested person is officially charged with a crime. The term "defendant" is normally used to describe a person who is in jail, and there is no way to determine if a person is a suspect or defendant unless you look at the records. To avoid confusion, I will be using the word "defendant" to describe the arrested person, even before the person is charged. There will be persons who will challenge the technical use of the words, and I am fully aware of the definitions. For the sake of simplicity, the word "defendant" will be used do define the arrested person.

All the members of the criminal justice family are familiar to me. I know their strengths, and I know their weaknesses. I know about drugs being planted on innocent persons, drug use and sale by law enforcement officers and their superiors as well as prosecutors and defense attorneys, theft of private property, extortion, rape, and death threats.

Many members of this criminal justice family are honest and brave and have sacrificed their personal lives for their community. Many times, these honest criminal justice family members do not remain within the family and find other professions outside the criminal justice system. Their consciences might prohibit them from doing the bidding of their superiors in order to get promoted or simply to keep their jobs.

IRS investigators carry weapons. I cannot think of any governmental agency which generates more anger than the IRS. The IRS enforces a tax code of 74,608 pages, which is quite an increase from 26,300 pages in 1984. [1]

When an IRS agent comes to lock down your business and start carting off your belongings (as they can do in what is called a "jeopardy assessment") I assume someone might pull out a gun, but that is rare.

According to Officer Down Memorial Page, four IRS agents are listed as having died since 1989 while on duty; one by heart attack, one struck by a vehicle, and two by automobile accident. [2]

I do not include IRS investigators, and their field investigators, within the criminal justice family as a subject of this book.

Some honest people remain in the family, and I identify some as friends of mine. At least five former members of the law enforcement family were employed by me. I asked one, "What percentage of law enforcement is corrupt?" His answer was sixty percent.

I have the utmost respect for those who put themselves in dangerous situations, life threatening situations, in order to protect the citizens. These are brave people and deserve admiration. The same enthusiasm should be used to expel the bad seeds of the family. I am not a flaming liberal, nor do I subscribe to Kool-Aid drinking conservative thought. We were taught to believe our parents, teachers, police, news writers, prosecutors, police, clergy, and politicians. These people tell you things because they want you to believe what they are telling you. They all have a motive, an agenda for wanting you to believe what they said. Some motives are honorable, some not. For the prosecutor, winning is all that matters, and the truth be damned.

This book is being written to be understood by persons who are not lawyers or part of "the family." The focus is mainly upon the statewide criminal justice. You will see federal and state similarities in references to federal cases. There are quotes from judges, lawyers, prosecutors, and case law which you should easily understand so you can learn the system, and secrets within "the criminal justice family."

There are moral and ethical pitfalls for each family member. The prosecutor is the head of the family, having more leverage over the other family members.

The prosecutor has more ways to push the agenda, which is a conviction. The prosecutor can also criticize another family member, but no one can criticize the prosecutor.

You will find many footnotes and many references in this book. I invite you to look at the bibliography and read some of my reference material. There are transcripts from trials, oral arguments from the US Supreme Court (justices chewing out lawyers), newspaper articles, website information, and copies of excerpts from writings and journals of highly esteemed judges, lawyers, and reporters. The copied text of court rulings, transcripts, and news reports are easy to read, so don't get overwhelmed with something which you might not be familiar.

After almost three decades of being involved with all aspects of the legal system, I came away with a view that the legal system, and specifically the criminal justice system, is a dirty, dirty business. It was comforting to see that many others, the judges, lawyers, and reporters, agree with me.

People who choose to join the family and stay in the family will probably lose their souls. You can be part of the family, but if you do not participate in the misconduct, you had better have thick skin if you want to survive in this family.

I have heard many stories from those on the street about misconduct by the dirty members of the criminal justice family. Many of the victims have these responses: "that this is the way it is", "no one will listen or believe me", and "no one will do anything about it."

This book will serve three purposes: to educate ordinary citizens (Joe Six-Pack), to get this project out of my head and onto paper, and to validate my experiences with opinions and facts expressed by judges and lawyers who agree with my assessment. If you want the truth, and sometimes be shocked at the lack of morals within this family, listen to a person who has been in the trenches. If you want to be entertained, and believe the cop is always right and the pretty prosecutor is always doing the will of the people, keep watching television.

I continue to communicate with current and former law enforcement officers, whom I consider friends. We have been on opposite sides of many issues, as well as the same side. They are my friends because they are hard core, honest, and know I am telling the truth. They will have a few strong words for me when this is done, and I will laugh.

You will now read about the job of each person in the criminal justice family, how they are associated with other members of the family, and why they are all in bed together.

THE CRIMINAL JUSTICE PROCESS, AND THE FAMILY

Crime Committed: Arrest at the Scene

If you are arrested at the scene of a crime, you, as the new suspect, can be served with a warrant while you are in jail, for the crime which was committed. To the arresting officer, there appears to be no question of guilt; the police "saw" the person commit the crime, and he will report that it was you who committed the crime.

If the police thought they "saw" you commit a crime at the scene of the crime, their observation and conclusion can always be questioned. This makes us think of a video representation of a crime; no one knows what happened before the beginning of the video. The cop might see a person attack another person but did know what provoked the person to attack; it could be a result of self-defense. A group of persons could be involved in what appears to be a crime, and the cop might arrest a person he thinks was the person within the group who committed the crime, making the cop an eyewitness. (The subject of challenging eyewitness accounts will be addressed later).

People can also be arrested at the scene of a crime as a result of police interviewing persons at the scene. Again, the police would be basing an arrest upon an eyewitness, and the eyewitness would have the same issues of having full knowledge of the event, mistaken identity, or mistaken auditory recollection (meaning what they heard, or thought they heard).

Persons at the scene of the crime could point out another person at the scene of the crime to be the person who committed the crime, with the purpose being to deflect attention from them or deflect attention from another person.

Many issues come into play at the scene of a crime.

Crime Committed: No Suspect Arrested at the Scene

What if a crime was committed and no one was arrested at the scene? An investigation must take place within the appropriate law enforcement jurisdiction (which is the geographical area where the crime was committed, like a state or county), and the investigators try to get information which will lead to a warrant being issued and have a person arrested.

A report is submitted to the prosecutor from the investigating law enforcement agency. The prosecutor can write up the warrant, or sometimes the law enforcement office can write up the warrant, and simply get it approved by the prosecutor. Years ago, law enforcement was authorized to write up a warrant and take the warrant directly to a magistrate or a judge to be signed. After the judge signed the warrant, the law enforcement official would make the arrest. Now, most jurisdictions have warrants presented only by a prosecutor. This keeps the prosecutor advised of warrants so the prosecutor can feel comfortable that an arrest will result in a conviction.

If the prosecutor would rather go before a grand jury rather than a judge for a warrant, the grand jury will listen to the testimony of the prosecutor and any witnesses called by the prosecutor. If the grand jury believes there is enough evidence to charge the suspect, the grand jury will return a "True Bill" which is printed on the form which lists the charges. This means instead of a warrant, there is an indictment, basically the same thing, and the suspect will soon be arrested and become a defendant after being arrested by law enforcement.

The Arrest

Law enforcement takes the warrant or the indictment from the prosecutor and arrests the person whose name is on the document. This person might be arrested while in jail, or on the street.

Getting out of Jail/Getting a Bail Bondsman

After being arrested, the new defendant will need a bail bondsman to get out of jail.

Research conducted revealed that the following states do not have a bail bond system, and law enforcement are charged with keeping up with persons out on bail: Massachusetts, Maine, Oregon, Illinois, Kentucky, Nebraska, Wisconsin, and Washington, D.C.

The defendant does not want to remain in jail until a trial, which could take years to happen. The defendant might call his lawyer first, if he has a relationship with a criminal defense attorney. If a defendant had a relationship with a criminal defense attorney, or knew one, this usually meant the defendant had been arrested on other charges and the defendant would want to use the same attorney. The lawyer could call the bail bondsman, who would call a family member of the arrested person to sign a bond. In some places, it might be illegal for attorneys to directly refer an arrested person to a specific bail bondsman, or a bail bondsman refer a person directly to a lawyer, but those referrals happen all the time. Defense attorneys are not supposed to share in the fee charged by the bail bondsman (a kickback) but the bail bondsman needs to show his appreciation. It is just kept quiet.

As the arrested person appears at the bond court at the jail, the prosecutor asks the court (the judge) to make the bond a certain amount. The bail bondsman can contact the prosecutor or look at a computer database to find out the amount of the bond after the hearing. Many times, the arrested person had been arrested before, and used this same bonding company for the same reason defendants usually use the same defense attorney. There is comfort with being familiar with the same persons.

The inmate/defendant can call the bonding company and tell them that he is in jail. Usually a family member will call the bondsman and say that their relative is in jail. The bond company will get the name and contact information of the person who will sign for the bond. The person who signs for the bond will come to the office of the bondsman, and pay the fee for the bond, which is usually ten percent (10 %) of the bond. If the signer of the bond does not have the entire fee, the bail bondsman will usually let the person make payments.

For example, a defendant might be arrested and charged with Assault and Battery of a High and Aggravated Nature, commonly referred to as "ABHAN" as abbreviated. The prosecutor will go to the jail during a time set by the jail for "Bond Court." Inmates, who have not had a bond set, will be taken to the court to appear before a judge. (Modern technology has made it possible for the judge to be in a different location, and the Bond Court is conducted by television connection.)

The prosecutor reads the charges against the defendant and asks for a bond of $20,000 for the defendant charged with ABHAN. If the judge agrees, this bond amount will be published on the jail website or a person can call the jail and find out the bond amount.

The bondsman will then contact the family member or person who will be signing the $20,000 bond. If the signer of the bond does not have the ten percent ($2,000) fee, the bond company will negotiate a down payment and take payments for the rest of the fee.

Roll Call

After getting out of jail, the defendant will have to appear in court 2 to 3 times over a period of a year or so. This appearance in court is called "roll call." Every couple of months, all defendants having open criminal cases in a county, or a certain jurisdiction, must appear in court usually on the same day.

The first time you go to court after being arrested is called your "first appearance." The defendant will be notified by the prosecutor of the date of the first appearance. Sometimes the defendant is given written notification of the first hearing after the bail bondsman notifies the prosecutor that the defendant is about to be bonded out.

On Roll Call Day, the courtroom is packed, hot, and smelly. Most defendants are poor, have poor hygiene, live in dirty conditions, have drug and alcohol issues, and are repeat criminal justice "family members." Usually, the purpose of the first appearance is just to see that the defendant had not run away.

A member of the prosecution office will be standing next to the judge with a roster of names, all to be called out by the judge or the prosecutor. The judge will identify the defendant by name and the defendant will walk to the front of the courtroom and stand before the judge. Sometimes the defendant will have an attorney who will go down front with him to stand before the judge. The judge might ask a few questions, and the defendant is announced as "present" and is free to go until the next roll call.

If the defendant does not have an attorney and tells the judge that he has no money to hire an attorney, the defendant will be directed to the Public Defender.

If the defendant is not in court, the prosecutor will make it known to the judge that the defendant had "failed to appear" and the prosecutor will ask the judge for a bench warrant to be issued for the defendant. When the judge bangs the gavel, and orders a bench warrant, the crowd groans because they know this will not be good for the defendant. The bail bondsman's work will begin.

There have been instances where the defendant went to the bathroom, came back into the courtroom, and never heard his name called. The defendant calls his bail bondsman, who has the list, and tells the bail bondsman that he (the defendant) did not hear his name called. If the bail bondsman was in the courtroom, he would have heard the name of the defendant, his client, being called, and heard the judge authorize a bench warrant for Failure to Appear. The defendant will have to get his lawyer to contact the prosecutor and get this worked out. Sometimes the defendant will go back to jail for a night, and a new bond is issued.

If the bail bondsman is smart, he will be at all roll calls, to make sure all his clients appeared. The bail bondsman needs to know as soon as possible if his client did not go to roll call, and that a bench warrant was issued. The bondsman must go arrest his client and put him back in jail to avoid having to pay the bond to the court. The prosecutor and the judge usually give the bail bondsman a good bit of time to find the defendant. Most cases are not big cases, and there is no big hurry to arrest the person. I will explain more about the bail bondsman a bit later.

Getting a Lawyer, Appearing in Court

The defense attorney (maybe a public defender if the defendant cannot afford a lawyer) files a motion with the Court soon after being hired. The motion is called a Brady Motion, named after a US Supreme Court case, Brady vs. Maryland (1963) in which evidence of innocence was withheld from the defense attorney by a prosecutor, and it was found to be unconstitutional. I suggest you go on-line and find the case and read the opinion. All evidence in the possession of the prosecutor which is relevant and material to the innocence of the defendant is supposed to be delivered to the defense after a Brady Motion is served upon the prosecutor.

After the defense attorney goes to the clerk of court with the Brady Motion, the attorney will hand copies of the motion to someone at the clerk office, and the clerk will time stamp, or clock in, the motion.

The defense attorney will then either leave a copy of the motion in the mail/document box of the prosecutor or have someone physically carry a copy to the prosecutor's office.

The Brady Motion

After receiving the Brady Motion, the prosecutor is directed to give up his file. This is where the sticky part of the case starts.

The biggest secret of the prosecutor office is that they can hide information that benefits the defendant. The defense attorney cannot go to the prosecutor and look through the file. The prosecutor will go through the file (at his own leisure) and pull out documents which he will allow the defense attorney to see. There seem to be no checks and balances as to how the prosecutor picks through the file, and what he decides to copy. Sometimes, the defense attorney can have a subpoena issued for different law enforcement agencies which contribute to the file, and this is more productive than getting information from the prosecutor. The prosecutor's file is a collection of reports from law enforcement agency investigations. The prosecutor's office does have "investigators", but they do very little investigating. The prosecutor's file is a repository of reports from various places, like a library.

The evidence obtained from the prosecutor is called exculpatory evidence. Let's break down the word so you will never forget it. The prefix "ex" means "not, or no longer". Ex-husband means he is not your husband. The word culpable means having guilt, or responsibility for something that happened.

So, evidence which is exculpatory is evidence which will prove the defendant is not guilty. The prosecutor would rather the evidence be called discovery, but not exculpatory evidence.

When the defense attorney files the Brady Motion to get copies of all exculpatory evidence, how does the defense attorney, or the defendant, know they are getting all the information that is helpful to the defendant? The only person who knows what is in the file is the prosecutor (who has possession of the file) and the law enforcement agency which supplied the evidence, including the investigation report and notes. An autopsy could be in the file, separate from law enforcement files, and law enforcement can use the autopsy findings to make a criminal charge. It is a clever idea to subpoena the doctor who performed the autopsy instead of issuing a blanket subpoena to the prosecutor or law enforcement. This applies to all sources whose reports are in the prosecutor's file.

The prosecutors will "cherry pick" the file to give the defense the information from the file, usually only evidence of guilt, which says "your client did this, we have the evidence, and your client is screwed."

The prosecutor's office is not in the business to prove innocence; it is in the business to convict. As an advocate of the public (the citizens of the jurisdiction), the job of the prosecutor is to have bad people punished. The prosecutor does not want to give up evidence in a file which will help the defendant, that would make the prosecutor look bad, and that showed he was not prepared to have the right person arrested.

Many times, that information is hidden, or removed from the file so the defendant and the defense attorney never see the hidden material.

The only check and balance with respect to the defense attorney verifying the exculpatory evidence (discovery) received from the prosecutor involves the defense attorney sharing the information with the defendant and a good (and I mean good) private investigator. Both the defendant and a good PI will know if there is compelling evidence against the defendant, or something is missing from the file.

Sometimes the defendant cannot afford to hire a private investigator because the fee for the defense lawyer took all or most of the money from the defendant. That sounds cold, but I heard that many times, in cases when I knew something was not right, and the defendant and his family said they could not afford me.

Good PI's Find Hidden Evidence

A good PI can determine what is missing from the file which the prosecutor gives the defense attorney. The main things to find are witness affidavits, and investigator notes. By talking with defendant, the PI will learn and/or find out who was interviewed by law enforcement. There is always a chance that a "missing" affidavit exists from a person whose statement will show that the defendant is not guilty and has a good alibi. The PI and the attorney must carefully listen to the defendant. The PI must then get in the street and talk to the family of the defendant, and all friends and associates.

If someone gave a statement to law enforcement and that statement is not in the discovery from the prosecutor, then the prosecutor is hiding something.

If the defense attorney does not want a private investigator, either he thinks he is smart enough to figure out how to defend the defendant, or (and this really happens) the defense attorney has a relationship with the prosecutor and convinces the defendant to take a plea (even when a good defense could find him not guilty, or exonerate). The defendant is caught in the middle and being railroaded straight to jail, or prison, by his own attorney.

In my book, *Don't Get Arrested in South Carolina*, the defendant paid a defense attorney $5,000.00, and the lawyer submitted a Brady Motion. The defendant hired me 6 months later. The lawyer told the defendant not to hire me. I asked to see the discovery material which the lawyer was supposed to have received from the prosecutor. The lawyer refused to let me see the file, so the defendant got the file and we found out that the defense attorney had gotten no file information from the prosecutor over the prior six months. The defense attorney did not want the defendant to know that the defendant was being strung along in an attempt to take a plea. Also, the defense attorney did not want the defendant to know that I knew the defense lawyer was corrupt.

I conducted a defense investigation in a death penalty case in which the defense attorney (a public defender) refused to use information which would help in the defense of the defendant. I found evidence which would have proved the defendant was not the only person involved in the murder.

The defendant described a car, and a person's name. I found the car (sneaked onto the property, hoping not to be seen or shot by drug dealers) and the defense attorney refused to use the evidence. The defendant and his family were quite disappointed, and the defendant was sent to death row.

I have seen enough to know how to smell a rat, and sometimes the rat is the defense attorney.

WHAT SUPREME COURT JUSTICES SAY ABOUT PROSECUTORS

Supreme Court Justices Define the Prosecutor

In the next pages, you will see role of the prosecutor defined by Justice Robert H. Jackson (1940), Justice George Sutherland (1935), and Justice John Paul Stevens (2011), as well as a bit of background from which these statements were made. These are the justices who best define the role of the prosecutor.

Justice Robert H. Jackson: Prosecutor Power

On April 1, 1940, an address was given by Robert H. Jackson, Attorney General of the United States, at the Second Annual Conference of United States Attorneys in Washington, DC. The entire text can be found in the Journal of the American Judicature Society, entitled "The Federal Prosecutor." The comments made by Attorney General Jackson apply to local prosecutors as well as federal prosecutors.

The following is excerpts from the address given by Justice Jackson:

"The prosecutor has more control over life, liberty, and reputation than any other person in America. His discretion is tremendous. He can have citizens investigated and, if he is that kind of person, he can have this done to the tune of public statements and veiled or unveiled intimations. Or the prosecutor may choose a more subtle course and simply have a citizen's friends interviewed. The prosecutor can order arrests, present cases to the grand jury in secret session, and on the basis of his one-sided presentation of the

facts can cause the citizen to be indicted and held for trial. He may
·dismiss the case before trial, in which case the defense never has
a chance to be heard. Or he may go on with a public trial. If he
obtains a conviction, the prosecutor can still make
recommendations as to sentence, as to whether the prisoner
should get probation or a suspended sentence, and after he is put
away, as to whether he is a subject for parole. While the prosecutor
at his best is one of the most beneficent forces in our society, when
he acts from malice or other base motives, he is one of the worst.

If the prosecutor is obliged to choose his cases, it follows that he
can choose his defendants. Therein is the most dangerous power of
the prosecutor: that he will pick people that he thinks he should
get, rather than pick cases that need to be prosecuted. With the law
books filled with a great assortment of crimes, a prosecutor stands
a fair chance of finding at least a technical violation of some act on
the part of almost anyone. In such a case, it is not a question of
discovering the commission of a crime and then looking for the
man who has committed it; it is a question of picking the man and
then searching the law books, or putting investigators to work, to
pin some offense on him. It is in this realm in which the prosecutor
picks some person whom he dislikes or desires to embarrass or
selects some group of unpopular persons and then looks for an
offense, that the greatest danger of abuse of prosecuting power
lies. It is here that law enforcement becomes personal, and the real
crime becomes that of being unpopular with the predominant or
governing group, being attached to the wrong political views, or
being personally obnoxious to or in the way of the prosecutor
himself.

The qualities of a good prosecutor are as elusive and as impossible to define as those which mark a gentleman. And those who need to be told would not understand it anyway. A sensitiveness to fair play and sportsmanship is perhaps the best protection against the abuse of power, and the citizen's safety lies in the prosecutor who tempers zeal with human kindness, who seeks truth and not victims, who serves the law and not factional purposes, and who approaches his task with humility.[3]

Below is a brief background of Justice Jackson.

"Jackson was born in Spring Creek, PA, and raised in Frewsburg, NY. With only a modest education and no college degree, he spent approximately 20 years as a successful attorney in Jamestown before going to Washington, D.C. Robert Jackson served in the Department of Justice as Solicitor General, Attorney General, and ultimately Associate Supreme Court Justice where he presided over a number of historic decisions including Brown v. Board of Education. While he was on the Court, he was appointed by President Truman to orchestrate, administer, and implement the trials of the major Nazi war criminals in Germany. At Nuremberg, he served as the Chief U.S. Prosecutor at the International Military Tribunal (IMT). Jackson created a trial format that blended the disparate precedent and procedures of four Allied nations; he coined terms for previously undefined felonies such as crimes against humanity and acts of aggression.

After Nuremberg, Jackson returned to the Supreme Court and continued to play a profound role in decisions that impacted a changing nation, including those involving Civil Rights, racial integration, and the religious rights of individuals." [4]

Justice George Sutherland: Defining a Prosecutor

This definition of the role of the prosecutor was made by Supreme Court Justice George Sutherland in 1935 as a part of the Schechter majority decision in the case of Berger v. United States, 295 US 78, 88.

[He] is the representative not of an ordinary party to a controversy, but of a sovereignty whose obligation to govern impartially is as compelling as its obligation to govern at all; and whose interest, therefore, in a criminal prosecution is not that it shall win a case, but that justice shall be done. As such, he is in a peculiar and very definite sense the servant of the law, the twofold aim of which is that guilt shall not escape or innocence suffer. He may prosecute with earnestness and vigor-indeed he should do so. But while he may strike hard blows, he is not at liberty to strike foul ones. It is as much his duty to refrain from improper methods calculated to produce a wrongful conviction as it is to use every legitimate means to bring about a just one. [5]

Justice John Paul Stevens: Prosecutorial Misconduct

On Monday, May 2, 2011, Justice John Paul Stevens (Ret.) was a speaker at the Equal Justice Initiative Dinner which was held in New York City, New York. The subject of his talk was Connick v. Thompson (a Supreme Court case), addressing the excuse given by the prosecutor (Harry Connick, father of the entertainer) that "lack of training," with respect to releasing exculpatory evidence to the defense allowed the prosecutor to escape liability for misconduct by the prosecutor's office. Connick made up the excuse that the prosecutors on this case were not trained well enough to know how to turn over requested evidence to the defense. The excuse sounds stupid, but it worked, and Connick continued to be the dirty prosecutor.

Justice Stevens was a Justice involved in a case in 1983 (Oklahoma City v. Tuttle) in which the excuse of improper training was also used to excuse a law enforcement officer of liability for directly killing an innocent man. That case is referenced in Chapter 3, Law Enforcement.

Below are excerpts from the speech given by Justice Stevens at the dinner which was given in his honor:

"...[t]onight I hope to stimulate discussion about an important issue that is often overlooked. It is an issue that none of the opinions mentioned in Connick v. Thompson (2011), the recent case in which the Court overturned a judgment awarding damages to a man who had spent over 14 years on death row because the Orleans Parish District Attorney's office committed repeated and flagrant violations of their duty to turn over exculpatory evidence to the accused." [6]

"In an extremely thoughtful and well researched book entitled "Peculiar Institution," Professor David Garland explained that a principal explanation for the survival of the death penalty in America, when it has been abolished in most civilized jurisdictions, relates to reliance on local rather than a more centralized decision-making in law enforcement.

Locally elected prosecutors may qualify for higher office by convicting vicious criminals and governors may lose any chance to become president if they are responsible for an erroneous decision to grant clemency."

"In a democracy where local judges and prosecutors are chosen by popular election, the interest in effective law enforcement that helped elect Richard Nixon and motivated campaigns to impeach Earl Warren, creates a problem of imbalanced incentives that ought to be addressed at the state and national level." [7]

Evidently these three Supreme Court justices felt the role of the prosecutor was a very important role, which includes power and temptation for corruption.

Every law student has studied Sutherland's speech and Jackson's address as well. Many law students can recite parts of both, but many choose to ignore these justices when they become prosecutors.

Justice Jackson's attitude about the power of the prosecutor, using his office as his own vengeance machine, was a bit more cynical than my attitude, but I totally agree. I love it that Justice Jackson mentioned that the prosecutor could absolutely destroy an innocent person, and would, just because he wanted to, and that the prosecutor could make it happen.   Justice Jackson was not dreaming of things which could happen; he was making note of things he had seen happen or else he would not have mentioned this unlawful activity of a dirty prosecutor.

Prosecutors Use Vengeance

A simple accusation disguised as a question to a neighbor ("Did you know Mr. Smith was watching child pornography?") can be used to start a rumor which will eventually get back to "Mr. Smith." I have defended innocent people who were found not guilty, but most people think that a person found not guilty is still guilty because he "had to be guilty of something" if he was arrested. Maybe the defendant got off on a "technicality." Still, the reputation is damaged, and the prosecutor is happy. Vengeance can be a motivator in arrests and convictions.

Senator Ted Stevens

Senator Ted Stevens (R-Alaska) was charged with crimes involving bribery and kickbacks just before his re-election and the 2008 election of Barack Obama. Stevens almost won his election even after being found guilty just before the election. Steven's election loss helped tip the balance in favor of Democrats in the U.S. Senate. The charges against Stevens were dismissed a few months into the Obama administration in 2009 when it was published that the prosecutors falsified documents and hid evidence which would have helped Senator Stevens. Attorney General Eric Holder ordered the conviction be thrown out, but the damage was done. The federal prosecutor, a black female prosecutor, kept Senator Stevens from being re-elected. This was helpful to the future President Obama.

As an aside, one of the young prosecutors assigned to this case hanged himself after former Senator Stevens died in an airplane fewer than two years after the guilty verdict was vacated. He was aware of his misconduct.

If the misconduct had not occurred, Stevens would not have been on that airplane, and the young assistant prosecutor would not have committed suicide.

Justice Sutherland tells us that the job of the prosecutor is to see that justice is done. The voting public does not want justice; they want convictions. Show me a prosecutor who wins many death penalty cases and I will show you a prosecutor who will be elected for a long time.

Foul Blows

Every person understands what Justice Sutherland meant when he wrote about "foul blows" to a defendant. Foul blows are unethical acts, including hiding evidence, bribery, intimidation, perjury, and blackmail. Foul blows are corrupt acts. Foul blows are acts of knowingly conspiring with law enforcement and other members of the prosecutor's office to obtain a false conviction to enhance the careers of the prosecutors and law enforcement, or another benefactor, such as happened with the conviction of Senator Ted Stevens.

After reading what Justice Jackson and Justice George Sutherland said, you should understand what the prosecutor is supposed to do, how he is supposed to conduct himself, and that his job is not necessarily to win, but to find the truth. If you think that a prosecutor is looking to find the truth and not simply to convict a defendant, you have been watching too much television and too many movies.

The prosecutor runs the show. The other four members of the criminal justice family act at the direction of the prosecutor, and they have relationships with each other as well.

The New York Lawyer's Code of Professional Responsibility makes it clear that public prosecutors, as well as other government lawyers, have different responsibilities than private lawyers. Ethical Consideration 7-13 states, *"The responsibility of a public prosecutor differs from that of the usual advocate; it is to seek justice, not merely to convict."*[8]

THE PROSECUTOR: INVESTIGATOR, ADVOCATE, AND IMMUNITY

The Prosecutor Wears Different Hats

Under the federal civil rights statute, 42 U.S.C, §1983, two types of immunity can be claimed by prosecutors: absolute immunity and qualified immunity. The immunity which applies depends upon the function the prosecutor, or at the time of the misconduct.

When prosecutors act as investigators or administrators, qualified immunity applies. Under qualified immunity, prosecutors are immunized unless the misconduct violated clearly established law of which a reasonable prosecutor would have known. When prosecutors act as advocates, absolute immunity applies. Under absolute immunity, prosecutors are immunized even when the plaintiff establishes that the prosecutor acted intentionally, in bad faith, and with malice. [9]

Prosecutor as an Investigator

The prosecutor has the title of investigator when he is working with law enforcement and other prosecutors before a warrant or indictment is issued. At this time, information is being gathered and the investigation is being coordinated to target an individual or individuals.

The prosecutor, acting as an investigator, has limited/qualified immunity against civil or criminal liability.

Law enforcement always has limited/qualified immunity.

Role of Prosecutor as an Investigator

Before a warrant is issued, law enforcement will discuss a case with the prosecutor, and the case will be in the investigative stage for both law enforcement and the prosecutor. A report will be sent to the prosecutor and the "evidence" will be examined to determine if there is probable cause in which to get a warrant or for the prosecutor to take the evidence before a grand jury.

The prosecutor does not know the validity of the evidence, but even circumstantial evidence will cause a warrant to be issued based upon the interpretation of "probable cause." Warrants can be used to harass a person (usually a person with a criminal record), intimidate a person into testifying (threatening to charge with knowledge of a crime and not reporting the crime, which is "misprision of a felony"), or ruin the reputation of a person as a personal vendetta.

Once the warrant has been issued, the professional identity of prosecutor will change from an "investigator" to an "'advocate for the citizens" (from investigator to advocate). The liability of the prosecutor changes too; as an investigator, the prosecutor has limited qualified immunity; as the advocate, he has absolute immunity, and can do or say anything with no consequences.

Role of Prosecutor as an Advocate

The prosecutor is an "advocate of the people" as he prosecutes a defendant, after the warrant or indictment is issued.

The prosecutor, as an advocate, has absolute immunity.

Law enforcement never has absolute immunity.

As an advocate, the prosecutor pursues a conviction, whether it is getting a plea agreement or taking the case to trial. All this is done after the warrant has been issued or indictment has been returned as a True Bill.

The role which the prosecutor plays determines the type of immunity which is given to the prosecutor. Yes, the prosecutor gets immunity regardless of his role; the prosecutor can do pretty much what he damned well pleases with absolute immunity.

Again:

If the prosecutor is in the role of the investigator, before an arrest, he has limited/qualified immunity.

If the prosecutor is in the role of the advocate, after the arrest and in the courtroom, he has absolute immunity.

A prosecutor neither is, nor should consider himself to be, an advocate before he has probable cause to have anyone arrested. [10]

"[t]he actions of a prosecutor are not absolutely immune merely because they are performed by a prosecutor." [11]

In the landmark case of Imbler v. Pachtman, the Court held that prosecutors are entitled to absolute immunity under § 1983.197. [12]

Imbler v Pachtman was a case decided in 1976. More about this case will follow. This case remains the lifeline to which prosecutors are tied, allowing them to not only be criminals in the courtroom but laughingly do so, because they know they will suffer no consequences.

The lifeblood of the prosecutor's office is based upon two things: CONVICTIONS AND IMMUNITY. A prosecutor needs immunity to get a conviction because if misconduct was used to get the conviction, the prosecutor needs a safety net. It is a roll of the dice by the prosecutor as to whether he will be caught, but if caught, immunity comes in and keeps him from being punished.

Absolute Immunity- No Accountability

In the landmark case of Imbler v. Pachtman, the Court held that prosecutors are entitled to absolute immunity under § 1983. Imbler was convicted of felony murder and sentenced to death following a trial in which the prosecutor knowingly used false evidence and suppressed exculpatory evidence. Freed by a writ of habeas corpus after serving nine years in prison, Imbler sued the prosecutor for money damages under § 1983. The action was dismissed based on absolute immunity, and the Supreme Court granted certiorari to consider the question of prosecutorial immunity.

As the Court had previously concluded in cases involving legislators and judges, § 1983 should "be read in harmony with general principles of tort immunities and defenses rather than in derogation of them."

Presented with its first opportunity to address the immunity of a state prosecutor in a § 1983 action, the Court began by exploring "the immunity historically accorded the relevant official at common law and the interests behind it." The Court found that the historical immunity of prosecutors was grounded on the same policies as the immunities of judges and grand jurors. "These include concern that harassment by unfounded litigation would cause a deflection of the prosecutor's energies from his public duties, and the possibility that he would shade his decisions instead of exercising the independence of judgment required by his public trust."

Finding the common-law rule of absolute prosecutorial immunity to be "well settled," the Court concluded that public policy supported the continuance of the doctrine under § 1983 because the threat of civil liability would undermine prosecutorial performance and constrain independent decision making. The Court anticipated that actions against prosecutors "could be expected with some frequency, for a defendant often will transform his resentment at being prosecuted into the ascription of improper and malicious actions to the State's advocate." In the Court's view, the potential flood of civil litigation would divert energy, attention, and resources from the performance of prosecutorial functions.[13]

The shocking issue is that the prosecutor knew that the evidence he presented was false, as did everyone on the prosecution team, involving law enforcement officers.

The best resources for essays about the abuse of immunity included in this book are from Margaret Z. Johns, Judge Alex Kozinski, and Ivan Bodensteiner.

Other sources are Supreme Court Justices as they question lawyers in oral argument, and in their opinions in cases such as Cone v Bell, Connick v Thompson, and Pottawattamie County v McGhee.

Remember, you cannot have a dirty prosecutor without having a dirty law enforcement officer. Most dirty acts performed by the criminal justice family members involve other family members to make the system work for them. Therein lies the incestuous secret of the family; no one will know because "we" are not telling, and even if you think you know our secrets, we have immunity.

One Court opinion stated that if a prosecutor was fearful of being sued, the prosecutor might be scared to present evidence and later find out it was false evidence. Wait a minute; isn't that the job of law enforcement, to furnish truthful evidence to the prosecutor? This enables both the prosecutor and law enforcement to present false evidence.

This change in immunity from investigator to advocate can be challenged because the investigation does not end when the defendant is arrested. Additional information surfaces after the time of the arrest and before a trial or plea deal. Law enforcement is the investigative arm of the prosecutor's office, and if the prosecutor uses information from law enforcement to arrest and ultimately charge a defendant, the prosecutor is the one who should be liable and inspect the law enforcement reports and determine if additional charges are to be made, if the investigation is complete, and if the information given to the prosecutor is true.

According to Ms. Johns," absolute immunity violates public policy" which basically means that absolute immunity is a slap in the face to all citizens who should be protected by their rights.

First, absolute prosecutorial immunity undermines the integrity of the criminal justice system. Second, it denies any remedy to the victims of the egregious abuse of government power. Third, it eliminates the needed deterrent effect that a civil remedy would provide, especially since other checks on prosecutorial misconduct are ineffective. Fourth, it hinders the development of constitutional law and the implementation of structural remedies to systemic problems. Fifth, absolute immunity is not necessary to protect honest prosecutors from vexatious litigation since the requirements for proving a cause of action and the defense of qualified immunity are sufficient to eliminate unmeritorious cases. And finally, absolute prosecutorial immunity introduces unnecessary complexity, confusion, and conflict into the law.

Moreover, as the cases discussed in this Article illustrate, the misconduct at issue does not involve grey areas of controversy over which reasonable minds might differ. The cases involve blatant and often criminal misconduct--manufacturing evidence, tampering with witnesses, suborning perjury. Certainly, prosecutors should not be allowed to claim that they violated clearly established law against such misconduct in reliance on the cloak of absolute immunity to shield them from liability. Qualified immunity provides sufficient protection to honest prosecutors exercising discretion in uncertain areas of the law; absolute immunity, on the other hand, protects those who deliberately violate the Constitution. Thus, overruling absolute immunity will not upset any legitimate expectations but will provide a needed remedy for willful violations of clearly established constitutional law. [14]

This paragraph above, written by Ms. Johns, is the best argument made against immunity.

Prosecutors and law enforcement know what is happening and what they are doing. If the prosecutor withholds evidence after having been served with a Brady Motion (to get the file from the prosecutor), and defense attorneys know there is information in the file which helps his client, the defense attorney can present this allegation to the court and file a Motion to Compel. The defense might get more information, and they might not. The prosecutor will claim it was an oversight (as he winks and nods at his associates, the judge, and all law enforcement officers at his side.)

In Burns, a mother reported that her two sons had been shot by an unknown assailant. When the police concluded that she was the chief suspect, the prosecutor wrongly advised them that they could seek a confession from the mother while she was hypnotized. The prosecutor then used that confession to establish probable cause for her arrest. When these facts were revealed, the trial judge ordered the "confession" suppressed and the prosecutor dropped all charges. Burns brought a § 1983 action for damages against the prosecutor. The action was dismissed on the ground of absolute immunity.[15]

On a state level, suits filed against a prosecutor must work their way to the Supreme Court, which means the case against a person or government entity will first be heard at the local level. A more confusing issue has come up because the nine federal appeal courts do not all agree with the same level of immunity the prosecutor will have when a prosecutor knowingly introduces tainted evidence which was obtained (from law enforcement of course) during the investigative stage of the process. This means the evidence would have been obtained before the warrant was issued.

The Third Circuit gave the prosecutor absolute immunity, and the Second and Ninth Circuits gave prosecutors qualified immunity. A judge can have immunity. In one case, Stump v. Spearman, the trial court ordered the police to forcibly bring an attorney into the courtroom. Even if the judge acted in bad faith or with malice, judges have judicial immunity. Judges have qualified immunity when making employment/personnel decisions.

Qualified/Limited Immunity

As was stated by Margaret Johns, as she quoted from Buckley:

Under qualified immunity, prosecutors are immunized unless the misconduct violated clearly established law of which a reasonable prosecutor would have known. [16]

Qualified immunity involves a few factors with respect to the behavior of the prosecutor; the acts must be in good faith, no malicious intent, and allows the person to use their personal discretion.

A prosecutor knows that one illegal or improper arrest can ruin the reputation of a person, especially a person of the community who has never been arrested. Even if the charges are dropped, or charges reduced as a result of a plea agreement, the defendant's reputation is shot. Such is the power of the prosecutor, but he cannot conduct this power game without the other members of the family working with him, and all being corrupt as well.

Immunity- The Vaccination Against Citizen Lawsuits

You might know that the prosecutor and police are protected from civil liability (being sued) unless it is proven that the official violated Section 1983, by depriving the rights of a citizen by the authority of the office, also known as "color of authority." Immunity is an important thing. If you are immune from punishment, you can do what you want. If you are immune from liability, you cannot be sued. Basically, the immunity that the prosecutor has during the investigation (before the warrant) is that he can do what he wants, or technically as a reasonable person.

History of Immunity from Margaret Z. Johns

In 1871, the United States' criminal justice system bore little resemblance to the system we know today. In the English common-law system, criminal prosecutions were primarily brought by the victim's family and friends,419 and the American system developed in part out of this tradition.420 But even before the Revolutionary War, the colonies had begun replacing private prosecutions with public prosecutions.421 Yet well into the nineteenth century, and despite the official establishment of public prosecutors' offices, the private prosecution of crimes remained a significant feature of the American criminal justice system.422 For example, in Pennsylvania, private prosecutions were common.423 Thus, "[p]arents of young women prosecuted men for seduction; husbands prosecuted their wives' paramours for adultery; wives prosecuted their husbands for desertion."424 In this system, the victims and their families often retained private lawyers to prosecute the perpetrators of crimes against them.425

Obviously, in this tradition prosecutors had a personal stake in the outcome and were far from detached and unbiased participants in the process. As one commenter observed, "At common law criminal prosecution adhered to the pure form of the adversary system; each aggrieved party retained his own counsel to prosecute his private interest."426 [17]

Until the late 1800's, many towns and counties could not afford to hire prosecutors, and those which did, hired new fresh lawyers who used the office more as a social vehicle, and were not very bright. Some persons became prosecutors and traveled from town to town, in a circuit. These prosecutors were not prepared to try the case and had little time to know enough of the case to be effective.

Citizens who hired private lawyers to prosecute cases for them did so in anticipation of payment from the defendant of a fine or damages. The prosecutor would share in the reward; thus, the prosecutor was motivated by money. The prosecutor was a hired gun, or maybe the whore of the court.

For example, an 1845 Kentucky case held that an attorney could be held liable for malicious prosecution for leading a lay justice of the peace into issuing a wrongful order for the sheriff to seize the plaintiff's dwelling. As the court explained, justices of the peace rely on counsel to prepare proper orders: It would be strange, therefore, if the attorney, by art and contrivance, the abuse of the confidence reposed, and prostitution of his profession, should procure from the Justices, from malicious motives to the defendant, an illegal and oppressive order by which injury accrues to the defendant, if the attorney could not be made liable for the wrong. It is contended, that this rule will expose attorneys to perplexing litigation, to the manifest injury of the profession. If it should, the law knows no distinction of persons; a different rule cannot, as to them, be recognized by this Court, from that which is applicable to others. Besides, this is a numerous class, powerful for good or evil, and holding them to a strict accountability, will have the effect to exalt and dignify the profession, by purging it of ignorant, meretricious and reckless members.[18]

Evidently my characterization of the prosecutor as the whore of the court was shared by a judge in 1845. I am in good company.

The idea put forth by Professor Margaret Z. Johns was that immunity was never a part of the law, and common sense shows that prosecutors should not be committing criminal acts (in conjunction with law enforcement) to prosecute a criminal. You either have the evidence or you don't. Stop making things up and do your job.

Indeed, far from being a "well-settled" doctrine in 1871, there is not one single case adopting any form of prosecutorial immunity until many years later. Instead the defense of prosecutorial immunity developed two to three decades after the adoption of § 1983 as the office of the public prosecutor developed, but the courts split on whether absolute or qualified immunity applied. [19]

As time went by, prosecutors were given more and more advantages and latitude with respect to immunity. Remember, a dirty prosecutor needs dirty law enforcement to get the dirty evidence to prosecute the case.

This dirty evidence is presented as probable cause to get a warrant, or an indictment. Below is an example of a dirty prosecutor, dirty assistants, and dirty law enforcement:

For example, in 1908 the Supreme Court of California held that a complaint stated a cause of action for malicious prosecution against the district attorney by alleging that he had conspired with the deputy district attorney and sheriff to falsely charge the plaintiff with a crime and that he had convicted the plaintiff by procuring false evidence and intimidating the jury. The defendants contended no action would lie because the plaintiff had been convicted, and thus probable cause had been met. The court rejected this argument stating:

Certainly, if a man has procured an unjust judgment by the knowing use of false and perjured testimony, he has perpetrated a great private wrong against his adversary. If that judgment is in the form of a judgment of criminal conviction, it would be obnoxious to every one's sense of right and justice to say that, because the infamy had been successful to the result of a conviction, the probable cause for the prosecution was thus conclusively established against a man who had thus been doubly wronged.[20]

Somehow over the years, the courts have given the prosecutors more immunity than was ever originally intended.

For purposes of this Article, there were three relevant immunities in 1871: judicial, quasi-judicial, and defamation. First, judicial immunity extended both to public officials and to private citizens who were involved in resolving disputes, including "judges, jurors and grand jurors, members of courts martial, private arbitrators, and various assessors and commissioners."

As Justice Scalia has explained, "[T]he touchstone for its applicability was performance of the function of resolving disputes between parties, or of authoritatively adjudicating private rights." It precluded civil liability even where the defendant acted in bad faith and with malice.

It was adopted to ensure that those resolving disputes would act independently and without fear of consequences.   The Court explained in adopting the absolute judicial immunity doctrine in 1872 :[I]t is a general principle of the highest importance to the proper administration of justice that a judicial officer, in exercising the authority vested in him, shall be free to act upon his own convictions, without apprehension of personal consequences to himself. Liability to answer to everyone who might feel himself aggrieved by the action of the judge, would be inconsistent with the possession of this freedom, and would destroy that independence without which no judiciary can be either respectable or useful. As observed by a distinguished English judge, it would establish the weakness of judicial authority in a degrading responsibility. But absolute judicial immunity was not extended to prosecutors, who were liable for malicious prosecution if they acted unreasonably and in bad faith. Using a functional approach, judicial immunity would not apply to today's public prosecutors since they function as advocates, not independent adjudicators responsible for resolving disputes.[21]

Normally, prosecutors have more cases than they can handle. The prosecutors have a job; they handle all criminal cases in their jurisdiction and want a final solution. The only way to get these off the desk of the prosecutor is (1) a quick guilty plea (2) a plea bargain, lessening original charges or reduced original prison time, and (3) a trial. Trials take time, and this is time the prosecutor can be spending working on other cases. No one wants a trial.

I have known many prosecutors. I praise the prosecutors who abide by the law and take criminals off the street. If the truth is not the only motivator for the prosecutor, the morality of the prosecutor will be compromised, and the prosecutor will begin committing criminal acts in and outside the courtroom in order to get a guilty verdict, regardless of the truth.

I admire their work, when it is ethical. It seems bad news, and bad people, get more attention than good people; that is the case here. This book gives examples of how a good and honest prosecutor can become a criminal.

Prosecutors take information from investigative agencies (state, local, and federal) and prepare a criminal case against the defendant.

Much has been written concerning the job of the prosecutor. The job of the chief prosecutor, the head of the department, is political. The state prosecutor must be elected, and his approval rate is based upon convictions. If a prosecutor (and his assistants) loses cases and/or has charges dropped, the prosecutor will not be re-elected, and the assistants could be fired by the new prosecutor. Federal prosecutors are appointed by the President.

There is a bit of political lobbying in order for a lawyer to be appointed as a federal prosecutor. I have seen a federal prosecutor appointed who had tried very few cases in court (I believe it was fewer than 10). When he was appointed, he hired one of the best and smartest prosecutors who practiced   in state court, and the hired prosecutor ran the show.

INVESTIGATION, ARREST, AND THE BRADY MOTION

Getting a Warrant, and the Arrest

After the prosecutor and law enforcement believe they have enough evidence to get a judge to sign a warrant, and convince a judge that no misconduct by the prosecutor was committed during the investigation or preparation of the warrant, the warrant is signed and law enforcement takes a copy to go arrest the defendant. The prosecutor now wears the hat of the advocate, not the investigator.

Bail

The defendant will be arrested, placed into jail, and the defendant will wait for a bond hearing to find out how much it will take for him to get out of jail. The defendant has to go to the office of the bail bond company to sign papers within a day or two after leaving jail.

Brady Motion

The defendant has to go see his defense attorney. The defense attorney will file the Brady Motion with the Court and deliver a clocked-in copy to the prosecutor.

If the defendant cannot find a person to pay the fee for a bond, or transfer money to the person signing the bond, the defendant will stay in jail. The defense attorney can visit a defendant in jail, have a contract signed to become a client, and the defense attorney will file the Brady Motion while the defendant is in jail. The following is an explanation of Brady, taken from an article written by Margaret Z. Johns, entitled "Reconsidering Absolute Prosecutorial Immunity, 2005 BYU L. Rev. 53 (2005)".

This publication will be used several times as a reference. I suggest you access this article.

In the landmark case of Brady v. Maryland,669 the Supreme Court held that "the suppression by the prosecution of evidence favorable to an accused upon request violates due process where the evidence is material either to guilt or to punishment, irrespective of the good faith or bad faith of the prosecution."670 Unfortunately, Brady violations are one of the most common forms--if not the most common form--of prosecutorial misconduct, yet discipline is rarely imposed. [22]

Violation of Brady: John Thompson

The Supreme Court overturned a lower court decision, in which John Thompson was compensated for the years he was in prison as a result of prosecutorial misconduct by Harry Connick's prosecutor's office. Connick's office withheld evidence from the defense which would have proved the innocence of the defendant, Thompson. Justice Thomas wrote the decision and asserted that there was only one single Brady violation, and that the prosecutor's office was only liable for "failure to train." Justice Thomas cares little for my opinion but wait and see what happens the following year.

Even the so-called "single Brady violation" that provided the center-piece of the Court's analysis included at least two flagrant violations. Prior to Thompson's armed robbery trial in 1985, the crime lab had tested a swatch of fabric stained with the robber's blood; the lab reported to the prosecutors that the perpetrator's blood was type B. Thompson's blood was type O. The District

Attorney for the Parish does not dispute that it violated Thompson's constitutional rights to withhold from defense counsel the blood-stained swatch and the lab report. The history of that withholding is disturbing.

Assistant District Attorney Gerry Deegan was one of the prosecutors in the armed robbery trial in 1985. On the first day of the trial he checked all of the physical evidence in the case out of the police property room, including the blood-stained swatch. But he then excluded the swatch from the evidence delivered to the courthouse property room. Nine years later, after learning that he was terminally ill, Deegan confessed to a friend, Michael Riehlmann, also a former New Orleans Parish prosecutor- that he had suppressed blood evidence in the armed robbery case. For five years after Deegan's death, Riehlmann kept that information to himself. Ultimately, in 1999, Riehlmann executed an affidavit in which he attested that during the 1994 conversation, "the late Gerry Deegan said to me that he had intentionally suppressed blood evidence in the armed robbery trial of John Thompson that in some way exculpated the defendant. [23]*

The prosecutor, Deegan, could not have been the only person in the case who knew that the blood-stained swatch of cloth existed. People in the lab knew about the cloth because they tested it. The lab knew that cloth was never admitted into evidence. Law enforcement officers had to have given the cloth to the lab to examine and test. Many people kept the secret because they wanted to keep their job. Law enforcement was just as guilty as Deegan. They knew the evidence they gave the prosecutor. Deegan should have named all the people who knew what he had done.

The fact that the cloth was not brought up by the defense is because Deegan kept that evidence from the defense and violated Thompson's Brady Motion rights.

Justice Stevens stated:

"An overzealous prosecutor might adequately explain the Brady rule while simultaneously making it clear that violations of the rule-if undetected by courts- will never give rise to discipline and may even be rewarded. Prosecutors' electoral incentives and the facts of this case demonstrate that such prosecutorial malfeasance is more than a hypothetical concern." [24]

Justice Stevens hit on two big points: (1) if the prosecutor does not get caught withholding evidence, in violation of the Brady rule, he will never be punished and will be rewarded if he wins the case (2) electoral incentives, meaning convictions mean votes, are a priority. The prosecutor wants to be elected continually.

Justice Stevens went on to discuss the lack of liability on the part of prosecutors and the office of the prosecutor.

Justice Stevens wrote an opinion on a death penalty case which was reversed because of prosecutorial misconduct. Don't get me wrong; I would not mind having public hanging for some defendants, but when a prosecutor, assisted and covered up by law enforcement, hides information from the defense, public naked flogging would be in order. Below is a synopsis of the case from the opinion written by Justice Stevens, along with a few of his comments.

Violation of Brady: Gary Cone

Gary Cone, a Vietnam Veteran, became a junkie during the war. The terror of combat made him escape through drugs. He left Tennessee as a flag-waving soldier. He returned as an addicted person running from his memories of Vietnam.

On the afternoon of Saturday, August 10, 1980, Cone robbed a jewelry store in downtown Memphis, Tennessee. Fleeing the scene by car, he led police on a high-speed chase into a residential neighborhood. Once there, he abandoned his vehicle and shot a police officer. When a bystander tried to impede his escape, Cone shot him, too, before escaping on foot.

A short time later, Cone tried to hijack a nearby car. When that attempt failed (because the driver refused to surrender his keys), Cone tried to shoot the driver and a hovering police helicopter before realizing he had run out of ammunition. He then fled the scene. Although police conducted a thorough search, Cone was nowhere to be found.

Early the next morning, Cone reappeared in the same neighborhood at the door of an elderly woman. He asked to use her telephone, and when she refused, he drew a gun. Before he was able to gain entry, the woman slammed the door and called the police. By the time officers arrived, however, Cone had once again disappeared.

That afternoon, Cone gained entry to the home of 93-year-old Shipley Todd and his wife, 79-year-old Cleopatra Todd. Cone beat the couple to death with a blunt instrument and ransacked the first floor of their home. Later, he shaved his beard and escaped to the airport without being caught. Cone then traveled to Florida, where he was arrested several days later after robbing a drugstore in Pompano Beach.

A Tennessee grand jury charged Cone with two counts of first-degree murder, two counts of murder in the perpetration of a burglary, three counts of assault with intent to murder, and one count of robbery by use of deadly force. At his jury trial in 1982, Cone did not challenge the overwhelming physical and testimonial evidence supporting the charges against him. His sole defense was that he was not guilty by reason of insanity.

Emphasizing the State's position with respect to Cone's alleged addiction, the prosecutor told the jury during closing argument, "[Y]ou're not dealing with a crazy person, an insane man. A man ... out of his mind. You're dealing, I submit to you, with a premeditated, cool, deliberate -- and even cowardly, really -- murderer." Tr. 2084 (Apr. 22, 1982). Pointing to the quantity of drugs found in Cone's car, the prosecutor suggested that far from being a drug addict, Cone was actually a drug dealer. The prosecutor argued, "I'm not trying to be absurd, but he says he's a drug addict. I say baloney. He's a drug seller. Doesn't the proof show that?" App. 107.

The jury rejected Cone's insanity defense and found him guilty on all counts. At the penalty hearing, the prosecution asked the jury to find that Cone's crime met the criteria for four different statutory aggravating factors, any one of which would render him eligible for a capital sentence. Cone's counsel called no witnesses but instead rested on the evidence adduced during the guilt phase proceedings. Acknowledging that the prosecution's experts had disputed the existence of Cone's alleged mental disorder, counsel nevertheless urged the jury to consider Cone's drug addiction when weighing the aggravating and mitigating factors in the case. The jury found all four aggravating factors and unanimously returned a sentence of death.[25]

While that petition remained pending before the post-conviction court, the Tennessee Court of Appeals held for the first time that the State's Public Records Act allowed a criminal defendant to review the prosecutor's file in his case. [26]

Based on that holding, Cone obtained access to the prosecutor's files, in which he found proof that evidence had indeed been withheld from him at trial. [27]

The lower federal courts failed to adequately consider whether the withheld documents were material to Cone's sentence. Both the quantity and quality of the suppressed evidence lend support to Cone's trial position that he habitually used excessive amounts of drugs, that his addiction affected his behavior during the murders, and that the State's contrary arguments were false and misleading.[28]

Although we conclude that the suppressed evidence was not material to Cone's conviction for first-degree murder, the lower courts erred in failing to assess the cumulative effect of the suppressed evidence with respect to Cone's capital sentence. Accordingly, the judgment of the Court of Appeals is vacated, and the case is remanded to the District Court with instructions to give full consideration to the merits of Cone's Brady claim.

It is so ordered.[29]

Justice Stevens accused the State of Tennessee of making "false and misleading" arguments to the Court. False and misleading, to me, is lying. The attorneys representing the State of Tennessee were lying to the justices of the US Supreme Court? You would think this was professional suicide, but lawyers standing before the Supreme Court, representing prosecutors, do not give a damn about the truth; they are there representing a dirty prosecutor, and must jump through hoops. The lawyers presenting the case before the Supreme Court are usually from the Attorney General's office of the state in which the case originated.

Cone's defense counsel portrayed his client as suffering from severe drug addiction attributable to trauma Cone had experienced in Vietnam and that Cone had committed his crimes while suffering from chronic amphetamine psychosis, a disorder brought about by his drug abuse. That defense was supported by the testimony of three witnesses.

Repeating from a few pages ago, this is how the prosecutor characterized Gary Cone.

Pointing to the quantity of drugs found in Cone's car, the prosecutor suggested that far from being a drug addict, Cone was actually a drug dealer. The prosecutor argued, "I'm not trying to be absurd, but he says he's a drug addict. I say balony (sic). He's a drug seller. Doesn't the proof show that?" App. 107.

The jury rejected Cone's insanity defense and found him guilty on all counts. [30]

Gary Cone was found guilty of the murders. There is no doubt he committed the crimes, but what the prosecutor did after that, in the penalty phase, was the issue which brought the case before the Supreme Court; an act of prosecutorial misconduct by not releasing exculpatory evidence which could have been used during the penalty phase.

Cone appealed the denial of his petition to the Tennessee Court of Criminal Appeals, asserting that the post-conviction court had erred by dismissing 13 claims -- his Brady claim among them -- as previously determined when, in fact, they had not been "previously addressed or determined by any court."[31]

While the new petition was pending, Cone did get a ruling that he would be able to review the prosecutor's file, citing the "State's Public Records Act". Cone's people found proof that evidence in the possession of the prosecutor was withheld from the defense, in violation of Brady.

On direct appeal Cone raised numerous challenges to his conviction and sentence. Among those was a claim that the prosecution violated state law by failing to disclose a tape-recorded statement and police reports relating to several trial witnesses. See id., at 114-117. The Tennessee Supreme Court rejected each of Cone's claims, and affirmed his conviction and sentence.[32]

For some reason, the judges in Tennessee felt the evidence that was withheld by the prosecution was not material, or relevant. The case was then brought before the Supreme Court.

Oral arguments are heard before the Supreme Court, and the opinion is handed down months later.

Below are outtakes from the oral arguments, including comments and questions made by the justices, and answers given by Jennifer L. Smith, who was defending her client (the prosecutors). Mr. Goldstein is representing Gary Cone.

It was stated that the crime was committed in 1980 (28 years prior) and Gary Cone did not get access to the prosecutor's file for 12 years.

Prosecutors who have been accused of misconduct do not represent themselves in court. They are being accused of something they did wrong, so they need to have a lawyer just like any defendant in a criminal case.

In the case of Gary Cone, who was accusing the prosecutors of misconduct for hiding evidence (exculpatory evidence), the prosecutor was being represented by the Attorney General of the State of Tennessee, and that lawyer was Jennifer L. Smith. Jennifer Smith tried to persuade the justices that no misconduct occurred, and that Gary Cone should be executed. The oral argument was heard Tuesday, December 9, 2008.

The Supreme Court returned their opinion: Cone's murder conviction stood. His death penalty sentence was vacated (thrown out) because the prosecution painted Cone as a drug dealer, and not a drug abuser. Cone needed treatment very badly after he returned from Vietnam. The lack of treatment resulted in the crimes he committed.

Many of you have never read a Supreme Court opinion or the transcript of an oral argument from the Supreme Court. If you become a bit familiar with a case involving prosecutorial misconduct the issues are simple. I would encourage you to read this case involving Gary Bradford Cone v. Ricky Bell (the warden). The case number is 2007-1114.

BELL VS. GARY CONE: ORAL ARGUMENT EXCERPTS

Cone v. Bell

Below are excerpts from the oral arguments of Bell v. Cone. If you have never read a transcript from a U.S. Supreme Court Oral Argument, you will find this fascinating. Jennifer L. Smith, an attorney working for the Tennessee Attorney General's Office, is representing the prosecutors who presented the case against Gary Cone.

JUSTICE STEVENS: Let me ask just one quick question: Is it your view that the evidence was deliberately suppressed or negligently suppressed?

MR. GOLDSTEIN: Deliberately suppressed, although it doesn't matter under Brady. There was -they turned over almost nothing, and this was the heart of our case. They knew that we were conceding that the acts had been committed, and our defense was one of insanity, and it was our only argument in mitigation of the death penalty.[33]

Goldstein made his presentation and was questioned by the Court. Now it was time for Jennifer L. Smith to defend the prosecutors who had hidden evidence.

JUSTICE STEVENS: May I ask -- let me get something on the table. Do you agree that the evidence shows that this evidence was deliberately suppressed?

MS. SMITH: Your Honor, I don't think there's been any -- any finding about the

JUSTICE STEVENS: But is there any explanation for -- was there any explanation for it other than the tactical explanation?

MS. SMITH: There's no explanation in the record, there has been no finding about whether the evidence has been suppressed at all in this case because both the district court and the Sixth Circuit decided as a matter of law that the materials –

JUSTICE STEVENS: It seems to be relevant because if it was suppressed for tactical reasons, it seems to me hard to say that the prosecution thought it didn't make any difference.[34]

Justice Stevens was going after Jennifer Smith, knowing that her clients were guilty of violating Brady, and she was relying on the fact that lower court did not make an opinion if hiding the evidence was on purpose (to get a conviction and sentence) or an accident. Believe me, it was not an accident, because too many people knew what is in the file and what had been presented.

JUSTICE KENNEDY: Do you think the prosecutor had an ethical duty to turn over this material?

MS. SMITH: I think that the material -- if the material -- if the subject was immaterial –

JUSTICE STEVENS: It's a simple question, yes or no?

MS. SMITH: I think that as a legal matter there was no -- no need to turn it over because it was immaterial.

JUSTICE STEVENS: That's not my question. Can you answer my question? Did he have an ethical duty to turn this material over?

MS. SMITH: I'm unaware of any ethical requirement that he turn it over, and I don't think that -- and certainly under Brady if it's not material, we don't think it was material, then it's certainly not required as a constitutional matter. And the reason is not –

JUSTICE SOUTER: You believe that the materiality judgment is yours to make, the State's to make as sort of a gate keeping measure? Isn't the materiality an issue for the fact finder?[35]

The fact finder is the jury. The prosecutor was deliberately hiding the statements, because the prosecutor said Cone was a drug dealer, not just a drug user.

JUSTICE SOUTER: Do you think that's a proper judgment for the prosecution to make?

MS. SMITH: Well, I think that probably a prudent prosecutor would err on the side of turning over matters that –

JUSTICE SOUTER: Right. And –

MS. SMITH: -- have some relevance.

JUSTICE SOUTER: Wouldn't -- wouldn't he err on the side of turning over the matters because Brady leaves the materiality judgment, like all materiality judgments, ultimately, to the fact finder?

MS. SMITH: Certainly ultimately it's left to the fact finder, but the prosecutor is -

JUSTICE KENNEDY: Well, initially Brady leaves the judgment for, furthering Justice Souter's point, to the attorney for the defense. You're saying that the prosecutor can preempt the role of the attorney for the defense in deciding what to offer to the court as material? And if -- and if -- and if -- even if the evidence is in a gray area, that's for the defense attorney to decide under -- under our Brady jurisprudence, as I understand it. Correct me if that's wrong.

MS. SMITH: Well, I think -- yes, I think the defense ultimately would make the decision how to use the evidence that comes into his possession.[36]

Smith was dancing again. She said the prosecutor decides what is relevant, then she said it was up to the fact finder, and that the prosecutor should err on the side of giving up the file. How in the world did she think the justices would not find her argument empty?

Brady says that anything in the file that is favorable to the defendant must be given up. The fact finder in this instance is the defense attorney, who would be the person to determine if the evidence is material to the defense. Justice Kennedy gave a stinging rebuke of Smith, implying that Smith was saying that the prosecutor can bypass the defense attorney in deciding about the evidence.

JUSTICE SOUTER: Maybe I'm being -- but Justice Breyer made the point, and made it, I think very clearly, that although that evidence was in, the argument here -- the argument that was made before the jury in this case is that the witnesses upon whom the defense was specifically relying, were witnesses whose account of the defendant's drug use came solely from the defendant himself. Given that fact, wouldn't it have been mitigating evidence to learn that other people, at times relatively close to the events in question, without being coached by the defendant, had concluded that he was a drug user? Wouldn't that have been mitigating evidence?

MS. SMITH: I don't think that it would have been material to —

JUSTICE SOUTER: We are not asking about materiality at this point. We are asking about the mitigating character of the evidence. Would it have been favorable to the defendant? Would that have been its tendency?

MS. SMITH: I think it added no more than -than what was already before the jury.

JUSTICE SOUTER: That was not my question. Was it favorable evidence? Did it have a tendency to favor the defendant?

MS. SMITH: No, not under his theory, and the reason is —

JUSTICE SOUTER: Then I will be candid with you that I simply cannot follow your argument because I believe you have just made a statement to me that is utterly irrational.[37]

I find this funny. Justice Souter just told Jennifer Smith that if she was using the excuse that the prosecutor "thought" the evidence in his file was immaterial, which is why he did not give the evidence to the defense, her statement was irrational. It did not matter if the prosecutor "thought" it was immaterial. The prosecutor lied; he knew it was material but he violated Brady just to get a conviction. The prosecutor then threw Jennifer Smith to the wolves (the Justices) to defend his blatant act of hiding evidence.

Don't you love it when a Supreme Court justice tells a lawyer that her argument is irrational?

MS. SMITH: Well, let me explain if I -- if I may, and the reason I say that it is not mitigating is because the -- the entire question in the defense and for mitigation purposes is the defendant's state of mind at the time of the murder.

There was already evidence that there was -that he was a drug user. The fact that he was a drug user doesn't say anything more -- or additional evidence of drug use says nothing more about his state of mind at the time of the crime than what was already presented. The question is not whether he was a drug user. The record showed it. It came out of the mouths of the State's own witness.

JUSTICE GINSBURG: But what about the prosecutor who said "baloney." He said the prosecutor -- the prosecutor says: The defendant tells you he was a drug user. Baloney, he was a drug dealer. The prosecutor deliberately tried to paint this man as somebody who had a huge quantity of drugs, which he did, and he was dealing in them. I mean the -the prosecutor tried to portray a man who was a coldblooded killer, who didn't have any blurred vision. And that line to the jury, "baloney" -- he says he was a drug user -- that, it seems to me, is exactly what the prosecutor wanted to do, which is to tell this jury this guy's a dealer; he's not a drug abuser.

MS. SMITH: I think that the prosecutor overstated in that portion of his argument, Your Honor. [38]

Jennifer Smith admitted that the hidden evidence should have been given up, and the prosecutor overstated his argument in the penalty phase, meaning he lied to the jury. The prosecutor had no evidence that Cone was a dealer.

This is how the prosecutor wanted to make a name for himself, but he was unethical. Smith was relying on erroneous rulings from Tennessee appellate courts to validate an empty claim.

Gary Cone's sentence reversal: Prosecutor Misconduct

Within the Opinion for Gary Cone, the following was found:

2. The lower federal courts failed to adequately consider whether the withheld documents were material to Cone's sentence. Both the quantity and quality of the suppressed evidence lend support to Cone's trial position that he habitually used excessive amounts of drugs, that his addiction affected his behavior during the murders, and that the State's contrary arguments were false and misleading. Nevertheless, even when viewed in the light most favorable to Cone, the evidence does not sustain his insanity defense: His behavior before, during, and after the crimes was inconsistent with the contention that he lacked substantial capacity either to appreciate the wrongfulness of his conduct or to conform it to the requirements of law. Because the likelihood that the suppressed evidence would have affected the jury's verdict on the insanity issue is remote, the Sixth Circuit did not err by denying habeas relief on the ground that such evidence was immaterial to the jury's guilt finding. The same cannot be said of that court's summary treatment of Cone's claim that the suppressed evidence would have influenced the jury's sentencing recommendation. Because the suppressed evidence might have been material to the jury's assessment of the

proper punishment, a full review of that evidence and its effect on the sentencing verdict is warranted. Pp. 469-475. 492 F. 3d 743, vacated and remanded. [39]

There are a few issues which you should take from this part of the opinion. The Justices stated that there was suppressed evidence. That was big. The Justices found (1) the prosecutor was guilty of suppressing statements (evidence) from Gary Cone's mother concerning his drug activity after returning from Vietnam which should have been turned over after receiving the Brady Motion, (2) the suppressed evidence would not have affected Cone's finding of being guilty, (3) the suppressed evidence played a role in the prosecutor's misconduct by allowing the prosecutor to tell the jury that Cone was selling drugs, and was a drug dealer, when in fact, the prosecutor knew what he was telling the jury was a lie.

At the end of the quote, you will see the words "vacated and remanded" which means the death penalty was vacated (based upon the suppressed evidence) and the case was sent back to the lower court for a different sentence; a life sentence.

Hiding evidence affected the sentence as well as the guilt. The misconduct on the part of the prosecutor, including making statements which would not have been made if he had given up evidence to the defense attorney, caused Cone to be sentenced to death rather than a life sentence.

The prosecutor, and the prosecutor's team, were dirty.

THE PLEA HIDES MISCONDUCT

Plea Agreements-The Criminal Case Enema

Plea agreements are the biggest "cover-up documents" of them all. A plea agreement will allow the prosecutor to take a weak case and avoid a trial or having to run the risk of misconduct being exposed in order to win. It allows law enforcement and prosecutors to have all their mistakes and misconduct ignored. It allows the defense attorney a chance to go to his next case, and the plea is advertisement for the next potential client. It allows the defendant the opportunity to have some of his crimes wiped away, but he needs a bit of leverage which will come either from the evidence in the prosecutor's file, or information from the street given by a source of whom the prosecutor had no knowledge or could not compromise. It allows the bail bondsman to close his file, and not have to chase the defendant. Plea agreements can help everyone.

If there is no plea, a trial will happen.

With all this being said about prosecutors hiding exculpatory evidence from the defense, who would trust any prosecutor? This question is hurtful to the soul of American citizens. As I have stated before, I have investigated cases for the prosecution and the defense. I have been in the fray. Most professors are just that, professors, and have book knowledge of the issues but have never had their professional life hang in the balance in a courtroom, arrested anyone, or considered personal injury during an arrest.

Prosecutor Listens to Private Conversation

I knew a prosecutor who listened in on a conversation, in jail, between a defendant (I believe it was a murder case) and the attorney for the defendant. The prosecutor flipped the switch to open the microphone and heard the inmate talk to his attorney. I investigated cases against that prosecutor's office, and I knew all the prosecutors.

After it was made known to a judge that a prosecutor was listening to a defense attorney meet with his client, the judge put a gag order on the proceedings. Somehow the news broke that the prosecutor had listened to the conversation (the jailer supposedly was there when the switch was flipped and witnessed the violation of rights) and the news was on television. The judge was angry and vowed to find out how the story got out.

The news reporter was subpoenaed but she refused to give her source. It was well known that the husband of the reporter was a retired federal officer, and "pillow talk" came into play. The judge put the pressure on the retired federal agent, and he revealed that the reporter/wife had told him the source; it was a defense attorney. Guess what happened to the defense attorney; he went to prison. Guess what happened to the prosecutor; he got a reprimand and I believe a short suspension. The prosecutor had moved to another office. The chief prosecutor was called before the Bar, and he got a reprimand, which made no difference to him.

Five Options for Dealing with Misconduct

The authors of the article in the Yale Law review gave 5 options in dealing with misconduct:

Common-law personal tort liability- rejected by Supreme Court

Personal tort liability under Title 42 USC Section 1983 (person cannot deprive rights under "color of authority"- rejected by Supreme Court

Municipal liability under Title 42 USC Section 1983 (as supervisor or policy maker) - recognized as possible avenue for compensation for defendant

Criminal punishment for prosecutor- has almost never been used

Professional responsibility measures- professional discipline by the state Bar

Review of Misconduct by Yale Law Students

What happens if the prosecutor is guilty of misconduct? Below is an excerpt from the Yale Law Review in 2011.

Given the Supreme Court's repeated endorsement of professional discipline as the appropriate vehicle for addressing allegations of prosecutorial misconduct, one might suppose that state bar agencies frequently sanction prosecutors. In fact, prosecutors are rarely held accountable for violating ethics rules. In 1999, Chicago Tribune reporters Maurice Possley and Ken Armstrong identified 381 homicide cases nationally in which Brady violations produced conviction reversals. Not a single prosecutor in those cases was publicly sanctioned. Four years later, a study by the Center for Public Integrity found 2012 appellate cases between 1970 and 2003 in which prosecutorial misconduct led to dismissals, sentence reductions, or reversals. Yet prosecutors faced disciplinary action in only forty-four of those cases, and seven of these actions were eventually dismissed. The most recent study indicates that depressingly little has changed since 2003, at least in California. The Northern California Innocence Project identified 707 cases between 1997 and 2009 in which courts made explicit findings of prosecutorial misconduct, 159 of which were deemed harmful. The Project's review of the public disciplinary actions reported in the California State Bar Journal, however, revealed a mere six--out of a total of 4741--that involved prosecutorial misconduct.

As these studies indicate, infrequent punishment of prosecutors cannot be blamed on a paucity of discoverable violations. Even when judicial findings of misconduct result in conviction reversals, disciplinary sanctions are almost never imposed against the offending prosecutor. [40]

State disciplinary authorities have the potential to rein in unethical behavior by prosecutors. They can only perform this function, however, if states adopt ethics rules with bite. [41]

Under Rule 3.8 of the Model Rules of Professional Conduct of the American Bar Association, the prosecutor is identified as an "Advocate" which is assumed the prosecutor is an advocate of the citizens within his jurisdiction. These are suggestions and not law. Lawyers are supposed to know and abide by the RULES put forth by the American Bar Association, but the American Bar Association cannot take the law license from a prosecutor or any lawyer. All punishment must come from the state, or from the US Justice Department if the prosecutor is federal.

These rules do not address the fact that the prosecutor is not always an advocate. During the time that the prosecutor and law enforcement are putting together information and evidence for a

warrant, the prosecutor is an "investigator" and not an advocate. The prosecutor becomes an advocate when the warrant is issued or when the indictment is handed down from the grand jury.

SPECIAL RESPONSIBILITIES OF A PROSECUTOR

Special Responsibilities of a Prosecutor (ABA)

Below is the text from the manual of the American Bar Association concerning prosecutors. These are suggestions, not rules, because the American Bar Association cannot disbar an attorney or prosecutor.

Rule 3.8: Special Responsibilities of a Prosecutor Advocate

Rule 3.8 Special Responsibilities Of A Prosecutor

The prosecutor in a criminal case shall:

(a) refrain from prosecuting a charge that the prosecutor knows is not supported by probable cause;

(b) make reasonable efforts to assure that the accused has been advised of the right to, and the procedure for obtaining, counsel and has been given reasonable opportunity to obtain counsel;

(c) not seek to obtain from an unrepresented accused a waiver of important pretrial rights, such as the right to a preliminary hearing;

(d) make timely disclosure to the defense of all evidence or information known to the prosecutor that tends to negate the guilt of the accused or mitigates the offense, and, in connection with sentencing, disclose to the defense and to the tribunal all unprivileged mitigating information known to the prosecutor, except when the prosecutor is relieved of this responsibility by a protective order of the tribunal;

(e) not subpoena a lawyer in a grand jury or other criminal proceeding to present evidence about a past or present client unless the prosecutor reasonably believes:

(1) the information sought is not protected from disclosure by any applicable privilege;

(2) the evidence sought is essential to the successful completion of an ongoing investigation or prosecution; and

(3) there is no other feasible alternative to obtain the information;

(f) except for statements that are necessary to inform the public of the nature and extent of the prosecutor's action and that serve a legitimate law enforcement purpose, refrain from making extrajudicial comments that have a substantial likelihood of heightening public condemnation of the accused and exercise reasonable care to prevent investigators, law enforcement personnel, employees or other persons assisting or associated with the prosecutor in a criminal case from making an extrajudicial statement that the prosecutor would be prohibited from making under Rule 3.6 or this Rule.

(g) When a prosecutor knows of new, credible and material evidence creating a reasonable likelihood that a convicted defendant did not commit an offense of which the defendant was convicted, the prosecutor shall:

(1) promptly disclose that evidence to an appropriate court or authority, and(2) if the conviction was obtained in the prosecutor's jurisdiction(i) promptly disclose that evidence to the defendant unless a court authorizes delay, and

(ii) undertake further investigation, or make reasonable efforts to cause an investigation, to determine whether the defendant was convicted of an offense that the defendant did not commit.

(h) When a prosecutor knows of clear and convincing evidence establishing that a defendant in the prosecutor's jurisdiction was convicted of an offense that the defendant did not commit, the prosecutor shall seek to remedy the conviction. [42]

To paraphrase, the job of the prosecutor is to seek justice, and if he sees anything that keeps the truth from being exposed, the prosecutor is supposed to correct the roadblock to truth and justice as written in the rules of conduct.

If a prosecutor is presented with information from law enforcement that does not show probable cause for a person to be arrested, the prosecutor is not supposed to conspire with law enforcement in order to create a story or make up evidence in order to have a person arrested.

The slow pace of Rule 3.8(g) and (h)'s adoption offers a second cause for concern. To date, only five states have adopted the provisions in full or modified form. Eleven other states are currently considering amending their versions of Rule 3.8. The remainder (thirty-four states in total) have taken no action. [43]

Some states actively discourage complainants from filing allegations of misconduct. Mississippi's bar association, for instance, goes to great lengths to warn complainants of the serious consequences that can result from filing a complaint. The bar association's website begins its appeal by reminding potential filers that "lawyers are human."

The website continues, "The lawyer [complained against] inevitably suffers from the accusation, regardless of whether any misconduct is ultimately found. But, if you believe the complaint is well-founded, by all means make it! A complaint cannot be withdrawn once it has been received in this office." Georgia discourages complaints in a different way by requiring prospective filers to go through a mediation program before deciding whether to pursue a formal complaint. The mediation program reflects a disciplinary system whose primary focus is private disputes between attorneys and their clients. In designing its disciplinary system, Georgia's bar officials apparently did not envision complaints concerning prosecutorial misconduct, which ordinarily would not be amenable to mediation.[44]

State disciplinary authorities, who are comprised almost entirely of lawyers, also exercise nearly unbridled discretion in deciding whether to pursue individual complaints. While every state will dismiss a complaint for failing to state a colorable claim, it does not follow that every colorable claim is fully investigated. Instead, a disciplinary authority may decide not to pursue a complaint as a matter of resource allocation or because a reviewing attorney merely suspects that it lacks merit. In some states, like Florida, an investigation may be closed even where ethics violations are shown to have occurred, under the theory that "[t]he investigation of a complaint frequently has deterrent value in and of itself." Furthermore, disciplinary authorities often conduct their proceedings in secret and require strict confidentiality from complainants. They may also decide to dispose of a case by issuing a private reprimand to the attorney involved. The lack of laypersons on hearing boards and review panels compounds the problem by creating the appearance of bias toward lawyers.[45]

Prosecutors know politics involved in the prosecutor office. It is not just the politics of getting elected; it is the politics of staying elected.

The American Bar Association, Rule 3-1.2 defines the Function of the Prosecutor

Standard 3- 1.2 The Function of the Prosecutor

(a) The office of prosecutor is charged with responsibility for prosecutions in its jurisdiction.

(b) The prosecutor is an administrator of justice, an advocate, and an officer of the court; the prosecutor must exercise sound discretion in the performance of his or her functions.

(c) The duty of the prosecutor is to seek justice, not merely to convict.

(d) It is an important function of the prosecutor to seek to reform and improve the administration of criminal justice. When inadequacies or injustices in the substantive or procedural law come to the prosecutor's attention, he or she should stimulate efforts for remedial action.

(e) It is the duty of the prosecutor to know and be guided by the standards of professional conduct as defined by applicable professional traditions, ethical codes, and law in the prosecutor's jurisdiction. The prosecutor should make use of the guidance afforded by an advisory council of the kind described in standard 4-1.5. [46]

Convictions Are Votes

Reducing the crime rate means votes for the sheriff, and state and local police. Those law enforcement agencies which are not elected are appointed by a person who was elected. Prosecutors, as well as state and local law enforcement, "serve the public" because when voting time comes around, the public servants need to have numbers to back up their claim that they should be re-elected.

This takes us to the fact that convictions mean votes. If a prosecutor cannot convict a high-profile defendant, he might be challenged by one of his subordinates, or a private attorney, when election time rolls around. When a governor grants clemency or allows a prisoner to be set free before serving out the complete sentence, and this former inmate commits a major crime of murder or assault, the governor will have to answer to this. As governor of Massachusetts, Michael Dukakis granted clemency to a prisoner, and this prisoner committed a major crime after being released. The name of the prisoner was Willie Horton. George Bush used the example of Willie Horton as an example of Dukakis being soft on crime, and it was death blow to the presidential campaign of Dukakis. Bush won the election and became president.

I need to repeat a quote from Justice Stevens, given as an address to the Equal Justice Dinner.

"An overzealous prosecutor might adequately explain the Brady rule while simultaneously making it clear that violations of the rule-if undetected by courts- will never give rise to discipline and may even be rewarded. Prosecutors' electoral incentives and the

facts of this case demonstrate that such prosecutorial malfeasance is more than a hypothetical concern." [47]

Do you ever wonder how any prosecutors aspire to higher office? How many US Congressmen were prosecutors? Mayors? Governors? Look it up if you do not know the names of former prosecutors who have been elected to higher office. their position?

PROSECUTORS FABRICATE EVIDENCE WITH LAW ENFORCEMENT

Pottawatomie v McGhee

On January 5, 2010, the following headline was printed in the LA Times written by David G. Savage:

Prosecutor conduct case before Supreme Court is settled

*Two Iowa men freed after spending 26 years in prison for murder had sued, saying prosecutors framed them. With justices signaling they might favor the men, the county settles for $12 million.*48

The two men were convicted in the death of a retired police officer. The defendants, after many years in prison, got a copy of their file and found out that the police and the prosecutors coaxed witnesses to implicate the two defendants, and ignored evidence implicating another person. A witness later recanted his testimony and the conviction was overturned. The defendants sued the county, the prosecutor, and the police. The prosecutor admitted working together with the police, but the prosecutor claimed that the police should be sued instead of the prosecutor.

The case went before the US Supreme Court.

A quote from David Savage's article, the following remarks were made by two justices with respect to the argument made on behalf

of the prosecutor, in that the police should be sued, not the prosecutor.

Justice Anthony M. Kennedy said that was "a strange proposition."

Justice John Paul Stevens called it "perverse." [49]

Let's put this argument on a level that we all can understand.

The defendants were suspects at the time the police and prosecutors coaxed the witnesses to make false statements. During this time, the case was in the investigative stage, and both prosecutor and law enforcement had qualified immunity, meaning they could not violate a law of "which a reasonable person would know." It evidently did not occur to the prosecutor and law enforcement that suborning perjury (asking a person to lie, regardless if they testify in court), witness tampering, obstruction of justice, presenting a witness who knowingly is giving false information, are all crimes which they had committed.

Oral Arguments: Pottawattamie

Below is an excerpt of Page 20 of the Oral Argument before the Supreme Court:

JUSTICE KENNEDY: You're basically saying that you cannot aid and abet someone who is immune, and that's just not the law.

MR. KATYAL: No, what I'm saying and what this Court's decisions have said is that absolute immunity doesn't exist to protect bad apples. It reflects a larger interest in protecting judicial information coming into the judicial process. And if prosecutors have to worry at trial that every act they undertake will somehow open up the door to liability, then they will flinch in the performance of their duties and not introduce that evidence. And that is the distinction between the police officer, who is liable, and the prosecutor, who is -- who is absolutely immune.

JUSTICE SOTOMAYOR: A prosecutor is not going to flinch when he suspects evidence is perjured or fabricated? Do you really want to send a message to police officers that they should not merely flinch but stop if they have reason to believe that evidence is fabricated? [50]

MR. KATYAL: Justice Sotomayor, we absolutely want to send that message. The worry is that allegations of wrongdoing, as this Court has recognized in Imbler and Van de Kamp, can -- can supersede that. And just to give you –

JUSTICE SOTOMAYOR: Am I right that none of the -- neither of the two prosecutors in this case were sanctioned in any way for their conduct?

MR. KATYAL: I believe that is correct, and I also believe that no ethics complaints were ever brought. That is, rather the Respondents went into Federal court seeking money damages instead of ethics violations and the like. [51]

Justice Sotomayor made a great point with her question; none of the prosecutors were sanctioned when it was learned they presented falsified affidavits, knowing they were false, and were conspiring with the police to make sure these persons would give the false testimony. The attorney for the prosecutor, Katyal, gave the excuse to Justice Sotomayor that the victims chose to file a lawsuit instead of reporting ethics violations.

So now everyone is immune from all their sins?

Don't you think that filing a suit against the prosecutors puts the Iowa Bar Association on notice that they just might want to look into the matter? Don't you think that the police agency which conspired with the prosecutor would want to know who the dirty cops were that got the witnesses to make the false statements?

The witnesses who gave false statements did not do so unless it was in their best interest. There was some give and take. Law enforcement controls this part of the game, the game of informants. This subject of informants and snitches will be addressed later in this book.

Justice Kennedy said, seemingly tongue in cheek, *"You're basically saying that you cannot aid and abet someone who is immune, and that's just not the law."*[52]

The prosecutors and the police knew the statements were false, and knew false testimony was to be given.

I see two issues here: (1) coaxing a witness to lie is not only fabricating evidence, it is suborning perjury, which is a crime (2) the monies paid to the former defendants will come from the coffers of the county. The taxpayers pay the bill. The cost of having the defendants tried, incarcerated, and the cost of the suit was a huge sum of money, and none of it would have been paid if the cops and the prosecutor had not joined together in misconduct and criminal acts.

Evidently the weak argument made on behalf of the dirty prosecutors motivated a settlement.

During a trial, the prosecutor has absolute immunity. In the Pottawatomie case, the prosecutor and the cops worked together during the investigative stage, which meant the prosecutor only had limited immunity, and the prosecutor said that even though they had absolute immunity during the trial, that gave them the authority to use fabricated evidence because they would be immune.

The hard part for attorneys presenting a case before the Supreme Court is that they are defending another lawyer/prosecutor for misconduct by the prosecutor. It is hard to believe that the attorney presenting the case believes their "client" is not guilty of the misconduct.

A PROSECUTOR'S LIE EXPOSED A YEAR LATER

John Thompson, Juan Smith, and Brady

Most persons know Harry Connick, Jr. He is the talented musician and singer from New Orleans. We also know that New Orleans has a reputation for crime and corruption. Guess who was the chief prosecutor for New Orleans, who was the prosecutor against John Thompson and Juan Smith, the two cases which went back to back in years to the Supreme Court? It was Harry Connick, the father of Harry Connick Jr.

Harry Connick had two cases before the US Supreme Court between the years 2009-2011. The cases were Connick v Thompson and Smith v Cain. In the first case, Thompson was convicted of murder and was given a 50-year sentence. A PI reviewed the file and found reference to a piece of cloth, called a "swatch" of cloth, which was not given to the defense team. Evidence showed that three different prosecutors had possession of the cloth. The blood on the cloth was found to have a blood type which was different from Thompson's. Thompson was freed after spending 28 years in prison. Thompson sued the prosecutor's office and was given a 14-million-dollar settlement. Connick appealed, and the subject of the award went to the US Supreme Court.

The court overturned the settlement which was to be paid to Thompson. Thompson got nothing after spending 28 years in prison as a result of criminal acts by police and the prosecutor.

The reason for the reversal of the award by the Supreme Court was:

Connick's office and the municipality of New Orleans had "failed to train" the prosecutors on the rule of releasing exculpatory evidence.

There was no evidence of a "pattern" of this behavior on the part of Connick's office.

Connick's office got away with lying to the Court. All prosecutors are lawyers. All judges and lawyers went to law school. They all knew about a Brady Motion, and all knew about exculpatory evidence. The truth is the prosecutor's office hid the existence of the cloth, and that cloth would have proved that Thompson should never have gone to prison.

What a lie, and an insult to Thompson. Thompson did not get a dime.

Justice Clarence Thomas wrote the opinion in 2009 which overturned an award of $14 million dollars to John Thompson for 28 years in prison. The Court said that this was a "single Brady violation". Again, here is part of the opinion:

Even the so-called "single Brady violation" that provided the center-piece of the Court's analysis included at least two flagrant violations. Prior to Thompson's armed robbery trial in 1985, the crime lab had tested a swatch of fabric stained with the robber's blood; the lab reported to the prosecutors that the perpetrator's blood was type B. Thompson's blood was type O. The District Attorney for the Parish does not dispute that it violated Thompson's constitutional rights to withhold from defense counsel the blood-stained swatch and the lab report. The history of that withholding is disturbing. [53]

It appeared that no fewer than 6 different prosecuting attorneys worked on this case, and we are to believe that none of them knew of the blood evidence?

This behavior is not evidence that prosecutors are smarter and more cunning than the rest of us; this behavior exposes the attitude of unchallenged power which the prosecutor enjoys.

Two Louisiana Cases of Misconduct

Even though Justice Thomas wrote in his opinion, and Justice Stevens (retired) wrote that the "single violation" by the prosecutor office of Harry Connick was part of the reason for dismissal, the next year, a case from the same prosecutor's office would reveal the pattern of prosecutorial misconduct.

Notice the case number of the two cases from Louisiana:

Connick v Thompson 09-571

Smith v Cain 10-8145

Notice the "09" as in 2009, and the "10" as in 2010? These cases were heard by the Supreme Court in consecutive years. The justices had to hear the scuttlebutt of two cases coming up from Harry Connick's office, and probably knew that Juan Smith's case was coming the following year while they were hearing John Thompson's case.

The arrested persons were Thompson and Juan Smith. Both were tried and convicted in New Orleans Parrish, Louisiana. The chief prosecutor on both cases was Harry Connick.

Connick v Thompson 09-571

Oral Argument, October 6, 2010

Opinion, March 29, 2011

Nov 6 2009- Petition for a writ of certiorari filed. (Response due December 10, 2009)

March 22, 2010- Petition GRANTED limited to Question 1 presented by the petition.[54]

Smith v Cain 10-8145

Oral argument, November 8, 2011

Opinion, January 10, 2012

Dec 20, 2010- Petition for a writ of certiorari and motion for leave to proceed in forma pauperis filed.

Jun 13, 2011- Motion to proceed in forma pauperis and petition for a writ of certiorari GRANTED.

Ruling 8-1 [55]

In the Smith v. Cain case, the issue of withholding evidence by Harry Connick's was being defended by the assistant district attorney from New Orleans. The defendant, Juan Smith, was convicted. Below is a news article by Adam Liptak with respect to the oral argument.

The case of Juan Smith was before the Supreme Court with the same Brady motion issue. This time a shooting took place. Five people were killed. A statement was taken from a witness. The original statement revealed that the witness had his head down and did not see the killer. This original statement was hidden from the defense. Again, Connick's office violated the Brady Motion, with the defense asking for all documents concerning the defendant. Connick's office hid the original statement because the defendant was later "recognized" after law enforcement showed a photo of the defendant from a newspaper clipping, planting the seed into the thoughts of the witness.

I assume the US Supreme Court could not go back and pay Thompson since the "pattern" of failing to disclose exculpatory evidence had surely been established. Connick's office had two cases before the US Supreme Court between the years 2010 and 2011 and both had to do with illegally hiding exculpatory evidence. It is not often that a single prosecutor's office has a case go before the US Supreme Court within two years, or ever. The pattern had been established, and if an investigation of Connick's prosecutor's office had been conducted by the Justice Department, I bet more cases of violation of Brady Motions would have be found.

Was Connick's office immune from prosecution, whether by limited or absolute immunity? Connick's office had the cloth before the trial, which would seem to fall under limited liability, as having not tested the cloth during the investigative phase. Again, many persons were involved on the prosecution team. Were they scared that the cloth would exonerate Thompson? Were they protecting someone else? Were they protecting themselves, or were they flexing their prosecutorial muscles?

Was Connick's office hiding under absolute immunity by being the advocate of the people to prosecute the person whom he thought was the killer? Was Connick acting in good faith? No, Connick was not acting in good faith.

Adam Liptak Comments on Juan Smith case

In an article written by Adam Liptak on November 8, 2011, Liptak reported and commented on Juan Smith's case.

WASHINGTON -- Donna R. Andrieu, an assistant district attorney in New Orleans, had the unenviable task at the Supreme Court on Tuesday of defending her office's conduct in withholding evidence from a criminal defendant. She made the least of it.

Her halting and unfocused presentation elicited one incredulous question after another. The argument culminated in back-to-back rebukes from Justices Elena Kagan and Sonia Sotomayor.

Justice Kagan said she could not understand why the Orleans Parish District Attorney's Office persisted in defending its conduct. "Did your office ever consider just confessing error in this case?" she asked.

Justice Sotomayor made a broader point about the office, which has repeatedly been found to have violated Brady v. Maryland, the 1963 Supreme Court decision that requires prosecutors to turn over favorable evidence to the defense.

"There have been serious accusations against the practices of your office, not yours in particular, but prior ones," Justice Sotomayor said. "It is disconcerting to me that when I asked you the question directly, should this material have been turned over, you gave an absolute no."

"That's really troubling," Justice Sotomayor added.

The case, Smith v. Cain, No. 10-8145, arose from a mass murder in 1995, when a group of men burst into a house in search of money and drugs. They ordered the occupants to lie down and opened fire, killing five people.

Juan Smith was the only person tried for the killings. He was convicted based solely on the eyewitness testimony of a survivor, Larry Boatner. Prosecutors presented no DNA, fingerprint, weapons or other physical evidence.

Unknown to Mr. Smith's lawyers, Mr. Boatner had said conflicting things in interviews with the police. Just after the shootings, he said he could not describe the intruders except to say they were black men. A few hours later, he mentioned "a black male with a low cut, gold in his mouth," a description that matched Mr. Smith and five other suspects.

Five days later, Mr. Boatner told a police officer that he had not seen the intruders' faces and could not identify them.

Ms. Andrieu said the failure to turn Mr. Boatner's statements over to the defense did not violate the Brady decision because the jury would have discounted them. Almost every justice appeared to disagree.

Chief Justice John G. Roberts Jr. said, "If you were the defense lawyer, you really would like to have that statement where he said: 'I couldn't identify them.'"

Justice Antonin Scalia said of the evidence, "Of course it should have been turned over."

As her argument wound down, Ms. Andrieu retreated slightly, saying that a prudent prosecutor might have voluntarily turned over the materials. "Today we turn over all of this," she said.

Kannon K. Shanmugam, a lawyer for Mr. Smith, was questioned only lightly. He said the Brady violations in the case had been flagrant and egregious. [56]

I wonder what Justice Clarence Thomas thought after ruling on the Thompson case only a year before, noting a "single violation" by the prosecutor overturned compensation to Thompson, then seeing the Juan Smith case come up within a year, have the same violation noted by Justice Thomas.

Why should he care?

MISCONDUCT AFFECTS VERDICT AND SENTENCING

Verdict and Sentencing

A different type of misconduct affects sentencing, rather than guilt. If a person is found to be guilty of the crime, he must be sentenced. In capital cases, involving death (murder), there is a guilty phase and a sentencing phase. After the person is found guilty of the crime, all "special circumstances" come into play, and these circumstances are presented to the same jury who found the person guilty of the murder. The jury probably had heard enough during the trial to make up their minds as to whether to vote to have the defendant put on death row, or a different sentence.

The prosecution will paint the defendant as the devil and make characterizations of the defendant which might not be true. The defense will present testimony that the defendant was influenced by outside forces, be it drugs, threats, abuse as a child, or other situations which make it look like the defendant was not acting independently. One such case was that of Gary Cone.

As you read earlier, part of the Opinion from the Court and exchanges with the judges showed that the guilt of the defendant (Cone) was not the issue; the issue was how the prosecutors portrayed the defendant to the jury during the sentencing phase. The prosecutor lied as they tried to present Cone as a drug dealer, and withheld evidence which proved he was an addict, having begun his drug use as a soldier in Vietnam. This misconduct by the prosecutor was the difference between life and death for Cone.

Prosecutors look good when the judge agrees with them, and the judge does not overrule a sentence. Prosecutors also look good when they enter a sentence of death (or less) and publish their goal in sentencing. They know they are "shooting for the moon" by overcharging many defendants, but getting a good sentence is the end game.

The drama is the sentencing phase, where the lawyers, as actors (thespians to those who went to private school), pull on every emotional string they can find to get what they want. If the prosecutor can "paint the defendant with a dirty brush" by claiming he was drug dealer or that he had some other immoral trait, it will damage the defendant in the sentencing phase. It will make the defendant look as though he could never be a contributing member of society. The prosecutor will use a lie to get the sentence he wants, and if the defense cannot refute the lie, it sticks with the jury.

It is the old quip of "when did you stop beating your wife" which is used to influence the jury.

ZEAL DOES NOT BREED MISCONDUCT

Justice Stevens, and Zeal

Let's address one word used by Justice Stevens; that word is "overzealous." Does this mean "too much zeal?" What is zeal?

Repeating part of a quote from Justice Robert H. Jackson, the word zeal is used in the context of a positive trait, not an evil motivator.

"A sensitiveness to fair play and sportsmanship is perhaps the best protection against the abuse of power, and the citizen's safety lies in the prosecutor who tempers zeal with human kindness, who seeks truth and not victims, who serves the law and not factional purposes, and who approaches his task with humility."[57]

Zeal is a trait a person has which can propel the person to accomplish a goal. Zeal is the fuel used to take a person to the goal. Zeal has a positive context. People do not attach the word "zeal" as the motivator which causes them to perform a criminal or unethical act.

Unethical acts performed by prosecutors are sometimes identified as "overzealous." This is an incorrect word to be associated with unethical acts performed by the prosecutor. A prosecutor might make a mistake, but it was not because he was overzealous. A prosecutor might perform unethical and criminal acts but having zeal does not describe the prosecutor.

Zeal might cause you to lose focus and make a mistake. The conscious and deliberate unethical act of hiding evidence and other acts of misconduct has nothing to do with zeal.

Would you say that Hitler had zeal? Stalin? Does a serial killer have zeal? No, and there is no zeal present when a prosecutor withholds evidence and lies to the court to get a conviction. The motivator of the immoral prosecutor is power, pride, or pure evil.

Does zeal cause prosecutors to pay off witnesses, destroying evidence, making false statements, and entering false documents?

These unlawful acts are referred by the court as being "overzealous." But what type of zeal is it that causes a prosecutor to break the law and violate a person's rights?

BAD PROSECUTORS WANT TO BE INVISIBLE

Winning Fairly

In the case of two persons who were arrested for selling $100,000 worth of heroine to an undercover agent, a conviction was reversed, and the prosecutor was accused by a federal appeals court of a major ethical violation. Two comments attributed to Judge Alex Kozinsky were:

"The prosecutor's job isn't just to win, but to win fairly, staying well within the rules...The government has strayed from this responsibility,"[58]

Henry Weinstein Articles Address Prosecutors

In an article printed in the LA Times on October 4, 1993, Henry Weinstein wrote, in part, about the case:

The U.S. attorney's office in Los Angeles has taken the highly unusual step of asking a federal appeals court to erase or at least soften a stingingly critical decision that accuses a prosecutor of a major ethical violation in a drug case.

U.S. Atty. Terree A. Bowers made the unusual request in a brief he recently filed in response to an Aug. 4 U.S. 9th Circuit Court of Appeals ruling. That ruling reversed the convictions of two people for selling $100,000 worth of heroin to an undercover drug enforcement agent.In a unanimous decision by three conservative judges, the appeals court said the guilty verdicts had been tainted by Assistant U.S. Atty. Jeffrey S. Sinek's "misstatements" to the jury, which denied *the defendants due process of law. The opinion also said that his superiors seemed to have condoned his misconduct.* [59]

Had this US Attorney no shame? Judge Kozinski blistered his colleague for misconduct and blasted the office of the US Attorney for knowing that the prosecutor was hiding information from the defense and lying about it to the judge. U.S. Atty. Terree A. Bowers submitted the brief to the justices begging that they remove the whipping they gave attorney by Assistant U.S. Atty. Jeffrey S. Sinek for lying to the court.

Publicly Identifying Corrupt Prosecutors

In a publication printed by the William and Mary Law School Scholarship Repository entitled Prosecutorial Shaming: *Naming Attorneys to Reduce Prosecutorial Misconduct*, written by Adam M. Gershowitz, the following excerpt was taken with respect to the case mentioned above:

A. Omitting Names: From the Supreme Court on Down, Justices and Judges Do Not Name Prosecutors Who Have Committed Misconduct

If misconduct is important enough to reverse the conviction of a criminal defendant, then it would seem sensible that the public and particularly the legal community should know the name of the perpetrator of the misconduct. Yet, courts often go out of their way to avoid publicizing the names of prosecutors. The United States Court of Appeals for the Ninth Circuit's decision in United States v. Kojayan is particularly instructive on this point. In an opinion by prominent Judge Alex Kozinski, the court in Kojayan reversed a conviction for conspiracy to possess heroin after it came to light that the Assistant United States Attorney had lied in open court about the availability of a witness and the fact that the witness had a cooperation agreement. In reversing the conviction, Judge Kozinski spoke in sweeping terms about how "lawyers representing the government in criminal cases serve truth and justice first." The opinion has been cited nearly one thousand times and is standard reading in some prosecutors' offices.

More noteworthy than Judge Kozinski's prose, however, is the fact that he initially named the prosecutor forty-nine times in the slip opinion but subsequently deleted all references to the prosecutor's name from the final version of the opinion published in the Federal Reporter. But Judge Kozinski did not act fast enough to permanently conceal the prosecutor's identity; the legal database LexisNexis® had already uploaded the original version of the opinion that included the prosecutor's name. When told about the original version being available on LexisNexis®, Judge Kozinski responded with surprise and "wince[d]."

Judge Kozinski is not alone in his desire to protect the identity of prosecutors who have committed severe misconduct. Although the United States Supreme Court has specifically stated that one way to discipline misbehaving prosecutors is to "publically chastise[] the prosecutor by identifying him in [the court's opinion]," the Court has rarely followed its own advice. [60]

Initially, within the opinion, Judge Alex Kozinski named the prosecutor who was criticized. The offended prosecutor, Assistant U.S. Atty. Jeffrey S. Sinek, convinced another prosecutor, U.S. Atty. Terree A. Bowers, to submit a brief to the Court, which was a plea to the court to remove the name of Sinek, stating that identifying Sinek by name would do "irreparable harm" to the career of the prosecutor. A new opinion was published, and Sinek's name was removed. But Sinek's name was found on a legal database printed earlier.

This brings up another angle about unethical and immoral prosecutors: when they are guilty of misconduct, not all the defendants are innocent. Misconduct allows guilty people to go free just because the prosecutor thought he could get away with misconduct. When a prosecutor does this to an innocent defendant, innocent people go to prison and the public pays for their incarceration. If the defendant is guilty, and is freed because of misconduct by the prosecutor, the vulnerable public has to live with a criminal back in the neighborhood. Either way, we all suffer.

A prosecutor can sabotage a case (for a fee) to allow a defendant to go free. You can figure out how and why that happens.

Can you believe this? A prosecutor commits a fraud upon the court, has a conviction overturned, and the dirty prosecutor runs crying to another prosecutor for sympathy. The second prosecutor enters a plea to save the first prosecutor from being identified in the opinion. What does this say about the second prosecutor? What does this say about the person who is the boss of the first prosecutor?

Judge Alex Kozinski: Prosecutorial Misconduct

Judge Alex Kozinski was an outspoken justice of the Ninth Circuit Court of Appeals (located in California). He has made many comments about prosecutorial misconduct in his opinions.

Selected quotes from Judge Alex Kozinski are below:

"Prosecutors hold tremendous power, more than anyone other than jurors, and often much more than jurors because most cases don't go to trial. Prosecutors and their investigators have unparalleled access to the evidence, both inculpatory and exculpatory, and while they are required to provide exculpatory evidence to the defense under Brady, Giglio, and Kyles v. Whitley, it is very difficult for the defense to find out whether the prosecution is complying with this obligation.

Prosecutors also have tremendous control over witnesses: They can offer incentives -- often highly compelling incentives -- for suspects to testify. This includes providing sweetheart plea deals to alleged co-conspirators and engineering jail-house encounters between the defendant and known informants."[61]

Judge Kozinski has written much about prosecutorial misconduct, and you can find more quotes from him on-line.

Eugene Volokh wrote much about the misconduct of prosecutors, as did Adam M. Gershowitz. If you want to study more on this subject, these are great sources.

Criminal Law: Judge Kozinski

Prosecutorial misconduct is a particularly difficult problem to deal with because so much of what prosecutors do is secret. If a prosecutor fails to disclose exculpatory evidence to the defense, who is to know? Or if a prosecutor delays disclosure of evidence helpful to the defense until the defendant has accepted an unfavorable plea bargain, no one will be the wiser. Or if prosecutors rely on the testimony of cops they know to be liars, or if they acquiesce in a police scheme to create inculpatory evidence,

it will take an extraordinary degree of luck and persistence to discover it--and in most cases it will never be discovered.

There are distressingly many cases where such misconduct has been documented, but I will mention just three to illustrate the point. The first is United States v. Stevens, the prosecution of Ted Stevens, the longest serving Republican Senator in history. Senator Stevens was charged with corruption for accepting the services of a building contractor and paying him far below market price--essentially a bribe. The government's case hinged on the testimony of the contractor, but the government failed to disclose the initial statement the contractor made to the FBI that he was probably overpaid for the services. The government also failed to disclose that the contractor was under investigation for unrelated crimes and thus had good reason to curry favor with the authorities.

Stevens was convicted just a week before he stood for re-election and in the wake of the conviction, he was narrowly defeated, changing the balance of power in the Senate. The government's perfidy came to light when a brave FBI agent by the name of Chad Joy blew the whistle on the government's knowing concealment of exculpatory evidence. Did the government react in horror at having been caught with its hands in the cookie jar? Did Justice Department lawyers rend their garments and place ashes on their head to mourn this violation of their most fundamental duty of candor and fairness? No way no how. Instead, the government argued strenuously that its ill-gotten conviction should stand because boys will be boys and the evidence wasn't material to the case anyway. [62]

CONFIDENTIAL INFORMANTS, OR CI'S, AND SNITCHES

Another Form of Misconduct

Another form of misconduct performed on the part of the prosecutor is the use of tainted evidence presented by jail house informants. These informants are commonly referred to as snitches.

In California, the Los Angeles County Grand Jury reported that from 1979–90, "The Los Angeles County District Attorney's Office failed to fulfill the ethical responsibilities required of a public prosecutor by its deliberate and informed declination to take the action necessary to curtail the misuse of jail house informant testimony."[63]

Informants, or CI's, or snitches are a huge part of the criminal justice system, used by prosecutors and law enforcement alike. Most "private" sessions with the informant are held with law enforcement. Below are excerpts from an article by Ryan Blistein, published on November 25, 2009. Mr. Blistein uses an essay Snitching: Criminal Informants and the Erosion of American Justice, Alexandra Natapoff *as a reference in many parts of his article. I will further discuss snitches as they relate to law enforcement and prosecutors jointly and individually.* [64]

This is one more subject involving the prosecutor, and this one has a major impact upon convictions of drug cases, but the prosecutor is not the most influential in this matter; it is the snitch.According to an essay by Alexandra Natapoff entitled *Snitching: The Institutional and Communal Consequences,* Ms. Natapoff gives her insight into the institution of snitching (versus using the name "informant").   Ms. Natapoff is a professor of law at Loyola University, Los Angeles, CA, and a former Public Defender in Baltimore, MD.

Although this essay paints the snitch as the lowest form of scum ever to breathe, she did not deny the necessity of the snitch in crime solving, especially for drug cases. The experience of Ms. Natapoff gives us statistics and makes the case that snitches are a destructive part of the criminal justice system. I have a major disagreement with much of her opinion, and I base my opinion upon my experience being "on the street" and knowing the mindset of the snitch. The destructive part of the institution of the snitch is that the snitch brings out the worst part of the prosecutor, and especially law enforcement. Snitches enable and encourage law enforcement to break the law.

The best time for the snitch to be used by the prosecutor is when the snitch has been arrested and the current charge has not gone to court, or if the snitch is in prison. If a snitch is out of jail and has no pending charges, the snitch has little to do with the prosecutor. The most likely person with whom the snitch is involved is law enforcement. If law enforcement can make an arrest happen without exposing the snitch, the snitch will lead law enforcement to the probable cause, which the prosecutor will use in order to get a warrant. Law enforcement does not want to reveal their snitch.

Even the word "snitch" has a negative feeling. The word "informant" seems a bit more pleasant.

The informant seems to be a person who might be used one time, on one case, and that is it. Regardless of what you call them, people give up information for a reason, and most of the time it is a selfish motive; freedom from the system.

According to Ms. Natapoff, 20 percent get off the record cooperation credit, and 30 percent of the population is drug defendants. In 1998, a project was conducted and among 1,000 search warrants, 80 percent relied upon confidential informants. In other major cities, the percentage was upward of 92 percent.[65]

Most plea agreements are said to be transparent. If a defendant in a federal case cooperates or promises to cooperate with the government, the plea agreement can contain a "5K provision" which informs the court that the informant provided "substantial assistance," and you know what that means; that means the defendant is snitching on someone else in order to reduce his sentence. The defendant runs the risk of everyone knowing that he cooperated or snitched, but in reality, when big charges are dropped before a plea, you can bet the defendant made a deal with the prosecutor.[66]

According to Ms. Natapoff, the Department of Justice has guidelines of crimes which informants can commit and authorized by their "handler."

The prosecutor knows that their power diminishes when it comes to informants. Law enforcement can control the informant and can decide whether to let the informant get to the prosecutor. That gives law enforcement a wide area to work with the informant.

Ryan Blistein on Natapoff

The following are excerpts from an article written by Ryan Blistein with respect to Ms. Natapoff's essay. The article was printed on November 25, 2009.

"Sex, Beer, Heroin and Cocaine: How Prosecutors Pay Off Criminal Snitches"

All too often, prosecutors aid and abet the crimes of their informants. And that's just one disheartening outcome of American law enforcement's bungled dealings with snitches.

In Chicago during the late 1980's, the U.S. attorney was prosecuting a ruthless, religiously inspired gang called the El Rukns. Federal prosecutors were so dependent on incarcerated gang leaders to make their case that six informants were permitted to make a hedonistic mockery of the criminal justice system. Henry Leon Harris was one of several who had sex with a visiting wife or girlfriend in the U.S. Attorney's offices -- while guarded by Alcohol, Tobacco and Firearms agents. Harry Evans used heroin delivered by his mother, but wasn't penalized when he failed a drug test. Other snitches received money, beer and cigarettes or stole confidential prosecution documents. A prosecution paralegal engaged in phone sex with Eugene Hunter, a confessed murderer, and one informant called his supplier from a prison phone to complain about receiving low-quality cocaine. For a time, prosecutors covered it all up, but eventually dozens of verdicts were overturned.

The details of the El Rukn case may be extraordinary, but the gist of the story isn't. All too often, prosecutors aid and abet the crimes of their informants. And that's just one disheartening outcome of American law enforcement's bungled dealings with snitches. The use of criminal informants leaves innocents behind bars, puts informants at mortal risk, renders justice opaque and actually leads to more crimes. In Snitching: Criminal Informants and the Erosion of American Justice, Alexandra Natapoff, a professor at Loyola Law School in Los Angeles, described the shortcomings of how cops and prosecutors employ snitches and offers ideas for reform.

To Natapoff, the secretive, sloppy, unaccountable use of snitches ranks among the chief flaws of America's notoriously fallible criminal justice system. Questionable actions begin during the recruitment process, when police flip alleged criminals into informants without even charging them and, crucially, without a lawyer present. Even after counsel shows up, all incentives favor a deal that involves an agreement to snitch. The government ignores or reduces potential sentences, trading charges for information. The higher a defendant resides within a criminal organization, the more leverage he has and the more lenient a prosecutor might be, violating the "worse the crime, worse the punishment" principle of blind justice. Such practices have become so endemic, Natapoff argues, that decision-makers are desensitized to the profound compromises they're making with criminals, including cold-blooded killers.

As a law enforcement handler deepens his relationship with a snitch, he becomes reliant on the informant and sometimes bends the rules. Handlers may grant informants power over the direction of investigations or personally intervene when a snitch is at risk of jail time for unrelated crimes. One active informant in San Francisco sold AK-47s that killed a cop; others participated in the murder of civil rights workers and worked as professional hit men for years at a time -- while under law enforcement supervision. The Department of Justice estimates that 10 percent of the FBI informant pool has engaged in unauthorized crimes, despite government knowledge.

Cops frequently use informants to gather incriminating information, skirting the need for warrants or avoiding privacy laws by having informants record investigative targets, sometimes in their own homes. Investigators take advantage of unsophisticated defendants, flinging them into perilous circumstances to snare bigger criminal fish. Last year, as ABC News reported, 23-year-old college graduate Rachel Hoffman was caught with a small amount of drugs. Without informing her lawyer or family, investigators employed Hoffman as part of a guns-and-drugs sting operation. The targets of the sting killed her.

The troubling results of snitching wreak havoc in many communities, especially low-income black and Latino neighborhoods. Because snitches can tell investigators only about what and whom they know, the creation of a few local criminal informants may cascade into a series of busts, charges and new snitches. In some neighborhoods, Natapoff estimates, nearly two-thirds of young black men are informants --

part of the reason behind an excessive drug-related incarceration rate among people of color. Snitching also begets community mistrust, leading to more violence. In Natapoff's revisionist view, the urban "stop snitching" movement represents a complex communal attempt to deal with that fallout of the phenomenon -- not, as depicted by most media outlets, a witness-intimidation campaign. White-collar informants benefit from advantages: skilled lawyers and target letters that serve as warnings of pending indictments. Yet the government's work with high-class snitches incorporates many of the same mistakes as its street-level work, from leniency in sentencing to close personal ties between agents and informants.

The use of snitches is accompanied by a stunning lack of transparency. A criminal informant agreement may be a "clandestine, black market version" of justice, in which cops negotiate their own plea bargain and leave no paper trail. State and local governments often have few rules regarding informants, with decisions made at the unsupervised discretion of police and prosecutors who fail to record key facts about snitches for fear they will appear in the discovery process when a case comes to trial. Natapoff believes that snitching, which drives legal decisions into the shadows, represents a retreat from the core purposes of law enforcement: examining culpability and condemning crimes in public.

The author doesn't advocate the wholesale eradication of informants from criminal prosecution. She's well aware that some cases -- particularly in the terrorism arena -- just can't be built without informants, and some horse-trading is necessary to induce cooperation. She does, however, offer a convincing prescription for snitching reform. Much of it involves beefing up oversight and regulation, increasing police accountability on informant practices and improving data collection and transparency in regard to that data by investigators and prosecutors.

Other ideas seem less practical, given that law-and-order officials in both major political parties dominate state legislatures. For example, Natapoff would require law enforcement handlers to report all crimes perpetrated by their informants, and she supports law professor George Harris' idea of publicly funded "defense informants" to counterbalance testimony by prosecution witnesses. Actually, though, many of her proposals that seem radical have already become law in some states, including informant reliability hearings (Illinois), the requirement of corroboration for informant testimony (Texas) and the provision of legal counsel for uncharged suspects considering cooperation (Florida).

El Rukn cooperators, like so many informants before and since, are more than mere tattletales who gave up on their criminal buddies. In flouting the law with such impudence after cutting deals, they shook the metaphorical hand of Lady Justice, lifted her blindfold and spat in her eyes. So, too, did their handlers in the Northern District of Illinois' U.S. Attorney's Office, who broke numerous laws in the name of justice for El Rukn's victims.

What happened in Chicago, however, is the result not just of despicable individuals but, Natapoff suggests, of a systemic problem in America's legal system, which too often uses some lawbreakers to prosecute other lawbreakers. Though she doesn't deign to offer a bulletproof plan to fix the situation, Natapoff does point law enforcers toward a way out of the vicious snitching cycle. If more of them chose that path, we'd all be better off. [67]

Informants: Personal Experience

With all due respect, Blistein's article reads like a book report, but he does challenge Natapoff concerning the recommendation by Natapoff that law enforcement handlers report all crimes committed by their informants. This lady was a federal public defender but has no sense of reality. Any conclusions drawn by Natapoff were made in a sanitary office. You must be in the street, eyeball to eyeball with these people, and wonder "are we gonna get our asses shot," before a person really understands informants.

I have used informants. I have paid informants. If you are looking for someone, an informant must trust you. When you are looking for fugitives, you pay who you need to pay.

As far as prosecutors and law enforcement using informants, this is usually a game best played by law enforcement. Law enforcement is the buffer between the informant and the prosecutor. Prosecutors do have investigators assigned to their office, and most have police credentials, but they usually do not extract the information, they make the deals after the information is obtained, usually by law enforcement.

Informants love to play one person against another to get what they want. This can mean playing the prosecutor against law enforcement. The cops worked hard to put a man in prison, only to see the man become an informant and have his sentence reduced. This frustrates the cops.

Informants Do Not Create Crime

Bad cops and bad prosecutors, who are inherently evil, will commit criminal acts regardless of the involvement of an informant.

Using an informant takes a person (and his crime) off the street. Crimes which the prosecutor (officially) and law enforcement (unofficially) allow the informant to commit are probably fewer in number than the arrested person.

Crimes committed by law enforcement (extortion, drug sales, selling stolen merchandise, and other crimes) can be committed without the aid of an informant.

Natapoff's views are very different from mine, but I did read her article. Most of her observations are correct, but her Pollyanna attitude is better suited in not giving advice.

I will defend the use of informants and dispute the moral decay which Natapoff contends is created by informants and snitches. Everyone knows the game, and how dangerous it is. The guys on the street know how to play games with law enforcement to get advantages, and the funny part is all players think they are smarter than the others.

It is the job of a good defense attorney or the PI to determine if the snitch is credible.

The world of informants is a dirty world. Much can happen, and much of it is bad. Very few prosecutors have been in the street; they went to law school because they were smart enough and made good grades in school and stayed out of the street. The criminals in the street, for the most part, did not make good grades, did not go to college, and have been in the crime business (called hustling) all their lives.

There is a vicarious feeling among law enforcement, even a wee bit of envy, that the criminals can live their lives without some of the pressures of supporting a family, being successful among peers, having to be polite, and basically being constrained by the work-a-day middle or upper middle-class life.

The prosecutors do have a bit in common with the criminals, unless the prosecutor is clean and moral. The life of the prosecutor could be filled with hypocrisy: prosecutors do drugs, steal, lie, and have affairs. Show me a weak prosecutor and I will show you a prosecutor who will compromise his morals, and believe me, the informant can smell a dirty prosecutor.

Prosecutors, and persons of authority, are not supposed to be abusing people and depriving people of their rights just because they are an authority figure. The fact that people were being abused led to the passing of the following law: 42 U.S. Code § 198

Informants who are not   criminals have been adopted into the "criminal justice family."

"1983 CASES"

What is a "1983 Case"?

Many of you have heard the phrase "1983 Case" but were not sure what it meant. It basically means that a person who has authority (usually a badge but could just be a position) cannot deprive a person of their civil rights. You can call it a bullying law.

I will explain in more detail below.

42 U.S. Code § 1983

The law which was passed, US Code 42 Title 1983 (commonly referred to as Title 1983), is supposed to protect the civil rights of Americans. This makes it illegal to deprive a person of their civil rights under the color of authority. In simple language, just because you have some type of authority over a person, you cannot deprive them of their civil rights as printed in our Constitution. Below is a copy of Title 1983.42 U.S. Code § 1983 - Civil action for deprivation of rights

Every person who, under color of any statute, ordinance, regulation, custom, or usage, of any State or Territory or the District of Columbia, subjects, or causes to be subjected, any citizen of the United States or other person within the jurisdiction thereof to the deprivation of any rights, privileges, or immunities secured by the Constitution and laws, shall be liable to the party injured in an action at law, suit in equity, or other proper proceeding for redress, except that in any action brought against a judicial officer for an act or omission taken in such officer's judicial capacity, injunctive relief shall not be granted unless a declaratory decree was violated or declaratory relief was unavailable For the

purposes of this section, any Act of Congress applicable exclusively to the District of Columbia shall be considered to be a statute of the District of Columbia. [68]

Depending on the function being performed, a government officer is either entitled to absolute or qualified immunity. Absolute immunity shields the officer from liability even though she acted in bad faith and with malice. Qualified immunity, on the other hand, protects the officer unless she violated clearly established law of which a reasonable officer would have known. [69]

History of Section 1983

Here is a bit of historical background which will help you understand the reason this law was enacted to protect citizens from persons "under the color of authority" from denying the citizens their rights under the Constitution.

Before the Civil War, the citizens were protected by the Bill of Rights from an overbearing federal government, and government officials, but not state officials. After the war, officials from the North were sent, during Reconstruction, to oversee many facets of life in the South. Since the passage of the Thirteenth Amendment outlawed slavery, combined with lawlessness of the Ku Klux Klan, federal law enforcement and lawyers were sent south to insure no one would be unjustly prosecuted or unjustly allowed to freely disobey the law.

The defendant (and other citizens) needed to be protected from over-zealous prosecution and from government officials acting "under the color of authority" to deprive a person of his rights.

The problem is there are no checks and balances to this power.Congress passed the Civil Rights Act of 1866, and reinforced this by passing the Fourteenth Amendment, which was to ensure due process (having a case heard in a timely manner) and equal protection under the law. In 1871, Congress reinforced the Civil Rights Act of 1866 by making it a law and identified it as Title 42 USC (United States Code) Section 1983.

Congress passed the law, the Fourteenth Amendment, including Title 42 Section 1983, to keep public officials from abusing the citizens. Nowhere in the law was there any immunity given to these officials. It was assumed that common law would prevail, and if these officials committed a crime in the performance of their job, they would be accountable. Why would a person need or have any kind of immunity to do their job?

Indeed, since the whole goal of the statute was to impose liability on state officials who violated constitutional rights, it seems doubtful that Congress intended to insulate officials who were violating civil rights by granting them immunity. [70]

THE ORIGIN AND ABUSE OF IMMUNITY

Immunity Examined

The first venture into legislative immunity was the case of Tenney v. Brandhove, 341 US 367, (1951) in which the Court held that legislator's immunity of free speech was protected.

Next came judicial immunity, which was handed down by the Court in Pierson vs. Ray, 386 US 547 (1967) stating that judges had absolute immunity.

Qualified immunity was afforded to police officers, governors, and other public officials "so long as they acted reasonably and in good faith."[71]

And lastly, prosecutors claim absolute immunity as they assume the identity of the servant of the public, having the power to commit crimes in the courtroom and never be accountable.

Thus, began immunity. In theory, prosecutors need to focus on prosecuting the defendants, and not be worried about being sued if they did something wrong which hurt the defendant, whether the defendant was innocent or guilty. The prosecutor had to show good faith. People had to trust the prosecutor, which meant they had to trust a lawyer. Didn't the prosecutor take an oath, as a lawyer or as a prosecutor?

(I have many lawyer friends, and they understand that the phrase "trusting a lawyer" is a bit comical.)

Police and other officials, in their official capacity, could not receive absolute immunity. Even with qualified immunity, some police and government officials are very well insulated.

It was not just the fact that an official would be liable, but the official could be sued, and the horror of tons of lawsuits would scare an official from trying to do his job as best he knew how. The only thing the government official needed to know was he would not violate any rights of a citizen rights "which a reasonable person" would know.

The words "civil rights" first come to mind with respect to the civil rights movement of the 1960's, but all citizens have civil rights not to be subjected to misuse of authority, which is why Title 1983 was made into law.

The symbiotic relationship between a prosecutor and other "family members" of the criminal justice system is simply incestuous; all other members of the family exist as a result of the creation of the prosecutor who gave birth to the four siblings, and the real relationship between the prosecutor and other family members is secret.

All members of the family benefit from one another, and the secrets kept from the public are the same as "family secrets" which neighbors never know. I will show how the head of this family relates to other family members. Many times, more than two members are involved in deals at the same time. The reward for the risk of exposure is power and money, and the risk hardly exists because no one talks as long as they get paid.

The news outlets act at the whim of the criminal justice system in order to get their stories. News articles printed about corruption within the "family"are a very small percentage of deals made and family members ignore (or act as if the acts are ignored) actswhich the public would find incredible.

Acts During Trial Preparation

A prosecutor will commit a questionable act in preparation for a trial, and even be involved in the investigative preparation with law enforcement before a warrant is issued. Although the judge, the defense, the media, and those in the courtroom witness the dishonest and criminal acts performed by the prosecutor, the prosecutor is not held accountable; no punishment and no fine. Those prosecutors who are punished are so few in number that people are shocked when it happens.

In many cases, prosecutors are criticized harshly by judges, as in Cone, Pottawattamie, Thompson, and the Ted Stevens case, but no prosecutors suffered. It is as if the appellate lawyer defending the dirty lawyer takes the beating for the dirty lawyer because the appellate lawyer is making excuses for the dirty lawyer/prosecutor, which makes the appellate lawyer look dirty. It is only a job. Getting chewed out by a judge is simply practice, getting your feet wet in the appellate court, like a rite of passage.

Persons of authority can deprive another person of his civil rights. This includes police, prosecutors, judges, or even a neighborhood bully. It is a crime to deprive a person of his rights, but where is the accountability? It is a crime for a person to deprive a person of his civil rights when the person in control is "acting under the color of authority". This crime is committed because of the adage "crime pays"; it is hard to catch the offender, and if caught, the punishment (or lack of punishment) is considered as risk versus return. If the punishment is less than the reward gained from the crime, then the only thing to determine is what return (ill-gotten gains) is necessary to justify the cost of punishment.

Corrupt prosecutors fall into this category of criminals, but who prosecutes the prosecutors? The prosecutor hides behind all the family members in order to keep the family secrets quiet and be rewarded in money and power.

The American Bar Association can only make recommendations. The state bar associations are politically oriented, as is any state disciplinary committee. Getting a prosecutor disciplined by a state bar association disciplinary committee hard to do. It is the equivalent of "the fox watching the hen-house."

Prosecutors do not care if they are accused of misconduct. Being accused of misconduct makes the prosecutor seem more powerful, because the prosecutor laughs at his accusers. The public wants a conviction. Even if there is an appeal, most of the time the name of the prosecutor is not mentioned in the pleadings.

The prosecutor's office is run as a business. They get taxpayer money to run the office (and other fees shared with court offices), and pay expenses for employees, supplies, janitorial services, and utilities as any business. They work within a budget. Their job is to prosecute persons who have been arrested and/or charged with a crime.

A prosecutor's office can also make money from a bail bond company if a fugitive is not apprehended within a certain amount of time (which will be explained later).

The prosecutor is usually an elected position. If the prosecutor makes the public believe he is doing his job by keeping the criminals off the street, then he will keep his job and continue to be elected.

Most citizens have no concern with judicial indiscretions committed by prosecutors. Persons who are concerned with the misconduct of a prosecutor (obstruction of justice, witness tampering, withholding evidence from the defense, bribery, perjury, presenting false testimony) feel hopeless because of the power enjoyed by the prosecutor.

Television and movies are not helping tell the truth. The media makes the prosecutor appear to be the savior by attacking a defendant and the blood sucking, money hungry defense lawyer. I cannot watch the court and cop shows. There are too many misperceptions. It is "Hollywood" and is rarely real.

Before the Civil War, local judges would appoint local lawyers to defend persons who had been arrested. After the Civil War, northern lawyers were sent south to prosecute southerners, and local judges would appoint these new lawyers to represent Southerners for crimes which the occupying North deemed punishable. The new defense lawyers knew that they were liable for mistakes made in their vigorous attempt to incarcerate these defendants. There was no immunity for these lawyers. If a person was found not guilty, or had charges dropped, the former defendant would sue the prosecutor.

These suits were said to have been a hindrance to prosecutors and made prosecutors concentrate on defending themselves rather than focusing on prosecuting in a "vigorous manner."

One lawyer was quoted, complaining he was being sued for more money than he earned prosecuting cases.

Disregard for Rules of the Court

A judge might make a ruling that the misconduct on the part of the prosecutor was a result of:

1. Being Overzealous- too excited

2. Overreach- stretch the truth

3. Disregard of the rules of the court/misconduct- tried to get away with misconduct

Judge's Opinions of the Prosecutor's Behavior

1. Overzealous

This definition of the behavior of a prosecutor is very misleading. The word overzealous comes from the word "zeal" which is an emotion which drives a person to perform an ethical act. Zeal does not describe the emotion that drives an unethical person; the emotion which creates misconduct is immorality.

Opinions by judges who overturn convictions use the words overreach and overzealous to describe misconduct on the part of prosecutors. This is a polite way of calling the dirty prosecutor a dirty, filthy, bastard. Remember, judges used to be practicing attorneys, so there is a bit of commonality.

2. Overreach

Here the prosecutor is trying to connect dots which do not connect; he lies to the court and makes assertions to the court that are totally outrageous. Maybe the judge will equate overreach as being creative.

3. Disregard of rules of the court/misconduct

The prosecutor knows he has absolute immunity in the courtroom. Even if he prosecutes a person by presenting evidence which the prosecutor knows is false, it is rare that you as the defendant will ever get a dime by suing the prosecutor. Why should the prosecutor care what the judge says?

Excuses: Oversight, Harmless Error, Improper Training

1. Oversight- the lie that the prosecutor and all on the prosecution team failed to see same thing

2. Harmless Error- the "mistake" would have made no difference, not relevant or material

3. Improper training- the prosecutor learned nothing in law school about criminal law

Excuses are Gold

The prosecutor will claim that their misconduct was a result of an oversight, as if the prosecutor forgot to do something, forgot to include something, or forgot to present something.

Prosecutors do not create a case or do all the work by themselves. Law enforcement officers give the prosecutor the reports and their files for the prosecutor to make the case. Law enforcement knows what is in the file. Law enforcement personnel who were involved in the case are in the courtroom during the trial. They know what is being presented as evidence and sees what the prosecutor is

presenting to the court and the jury. Law enforcement is not going to jump up in the middle of a trial and correct a prosecutor while the prosecutor is committing misconduct because the prosecutor and law enforcement want the conviction and are together in trying to get away with bad behavior.

Law enforcement and others on the prosecution team are with the prosecutor all the time, either in the office preparing the case or sitting at the prosecution table. They all have notepads to write notes to pass to the prosecutor during a trial. They see the prosecutor during breaks. There is never any oversight.

If a prosecutor fails to present all exculpatory evidence to the defense, the prosecutor will use the excuse of oversight. Again, the prosecutor is not alone in the office. There are clerks, assistants, and lower ranked prosecutors who are helping prosecute the case. Everyone knows what was given to the defense after receiving the Brady Motion. They are just hoping they will not be caught hiding something.

(1) Oversight Excuse is Perjury

Trying to use the excuse of oversight is perjury by the prosecutor. Are we to believe that all the people who supervised and worked on the case forgot the same thing?

A defendant cannot use the excuse of oversight for his criminal or negligent behavior. "I forgot to unload the gun," or "I forgot to apply the brakes" or "I forgot how strong I am" are not excuses used by a defendant. Oversight cannot be used by the defendant and should not be used by the prosecutor.

Prosecutors are not punished for oversight. This allows them to try to use illegal and unethical actions against a defendant to get a conviction. The banner in the prosecutor's office reads, "Win at all costs, do whatever you think you need to do, get the conviction, just don't get caught and allow the defendant to walk out of   the courtroom."

Oversight could be mean the prosecutor accidentally did the following things: (1) misrepresented the truth, (2) used his authority in a manner to intimidate, presented false evidence, or (3) evidence he knew was not accurate, presented a witness who he knew would lie for the prosecution, and more.

(2) Harmless Error

The prosecutor will claim that their misconduct was a harmless error, meaning that the mistake (whether it was intentional or not) was harmless in that if the "error" had not been made, it would not have affected the prosecution of the defendant, and the conviction would have resulted.

Here is a definition from the Federal Rules of Civil Procedure. Rule 61, Harmless Error, is below:

Unless justice requires otherwise, no error in admitting or excluding evidence--or any other error by the court or a party--is ground for granting a new trial, for setting aside a verdict, or for vacating, modifying, or otherwise disturbing a judgment or order. At every stage of the proceeding, the court must disregard all errors and defects that do not affect any party's substantial rights.[72]

(3) Improper Training

This is the big joke. What the hell were they doing in law school, and how the hell did they graduate without knowing about a Brady Motion?

This excuse is given by the corrupt supervisors of the corrupt prosecutors when the corrupt prosecutors are caught doing something unethical or criminal. Even though the prosecutor's office "falls on their sword," they are smiling as they do this. This excuse was given by the office of Harry Connick after his prosecutors (I believe there were 5 involved in this case) were found to have violated Brady by withholding evidence from the defense in Connick v. Thompson.

These prosecutors know the issues about Brady Motions. These prosecutors learned criminal law in law school and would not have been given the job in the prosecutor's office if the person who hired them did not think they knew a bit about criminal law.

HARMLESS ERROR: THE BIG LIE

The Theory

Prosecutors use the theory of harmless error to try to humanize themselves to the judge and present an "oops" to cover their obvious agendas. Prosecutors only use the theory of harmless error when they are caught committing unethical acts.

As is mentioned many times in this book, you should know that the prosecutor does not prepare a case in a vacuum. Others in the prosecutor's office work on the same case and know how the case is to be presented. If the prosecutor fails to give up Brady material (discovery to be given to the defense) or gets caught lying in a report or presenting a fact in an inaccurate manner, others in the office know about it and they are all praying they do not get caught.

Harmless Error

The federal harmless error doctrine was enacted by Congress in 1919 to combat a serious problem plaguing the criminal justice system. At the time, criminal convictions were reversed on appeal for such minor errors as the omission of the word "the" from the charging indictment. In fact, any technical defect resulted in reversal. Compounding this problem were defense attorneys who, knowing it would result in retrial, sometimes deliberately placed technical errors into the record or consciously allowed such errors to occur.

While such reversals would put a strain on our modern judicial system, the burden was particularly acute given the logistics of the early 1900's, especially with regard to communication and transportation. Congress responded to the problem by articulating what has come to be known as the harmless error rule. To be classified as harmless under the original rule, the error must not have affected the substantial rights of the parties. By doing so, the harmless error rule prevented the setting aside of convictions for small errors which were unlikely to have influenced the outcome of the trial. The rule was broadly written and applied to a wide variety of situations. While the almost infinite number of technical errors prevented the drafting of specific rules to cover every conceivable situation, the general wording of the rule left open the question of just how broadly it was to be applied.

Prior to 1967, courts held Constitutional errors could never be harmless. In cases where a defendant's federal Constitutional rights were violated, the reviewing courts reversed the convictions and remanded the cases for new trials free of Constitutional infirmity. Despite these early cases, in Chapman v. California the United States Supreme Court treated the issue of whether a Constitutional error could be subjected to harmless error analysis as a question of first impression. The Court answered the question by holding that under some circumstances the violation of a defendant's Constitutional rights could qualify as harmless error.

Finally, in 1991 the Court attempted to provide a general rule for guiding the determination of whether a particular Constitutional violation was subject to harmless error review. According to Chief Justice Rhenquist writing for the majority in Arizona v. Fulminante, the type of right that was violated determines whether the harmless error rule applies.

Constitutional errors characterized as trial errors are subject to harmless error analysis, whereas structural errors are not. [73]

The History of Harmless Error Rule

In 1906, the state of Missouri tried and convicted Bruce Campbell for raping a young girl named Willie Clark. During the trial, the prosecution presented detailed and convincing evidence of Mr. Campen's guilt, including compelling testimony from the victim, Ms. Clark. Ms. Clark explained that she came to stay with Mr. Campbell and his wife while traveling to visit her father and brother. She described precisely how Mr. Campbell returned to the house one morning when his wife was gone and raped her. As further evidence of the defendant's guilt, Ms. Clark told the jury about Mr. Campbell's attempt to conceal his crime by offering her money in exchange for not reporting his vicious violation of her.

In addition to the victim's testimony, the jury also heard the testimony of a neighbor who had seen Ms. Clark shortly after the attack. Although not an eyewitness to the actual rape, the neighbor observed Ms. Clark crying, "bareheaded and disheveled" shortly after the alleged rape occurred. A physician who examined Ms. Clark shortly after the attack provided further support for the state's case by informing the jury that her Perhaps even more damning, a law enforcement officer testified that on the day the defendant posted bond, the defendant admitted to him, "I have a notion to plead guilty." Based upon this evidence, the jury found Mr. Campbell guilty of raping Ms. Clark.

A CRIMINAL JUSTICE HANDBOOK

Despite this seemingly accurate verdict, the appellate court reversed Mr. Campbell's conviction. The reversal occurred not because Mr. Campbell's federal Constitutional rights had been violated, not because the state failed to proffer evidence on one of the elements of rape and not because the evidence was insufficient to support the conviction. Instead, the appellate court reversed

Mr. Campbell's conviction merely because the language at the end of the charging indictment alleged that the rape occurred "against the peace and dignity of state" rather than the required "against the peace and dignity of the state."

Prior to the advent of the harmless error rule, results such as the one just described occurred all too often. Because a conviction had to be achieved in an error-free trial, the threat of convictions being reversed on such minor technicalities was great. Regrettably, the error-free conviction requirement reduced some criminal trials to nothing more than games for planting the seeds of reversible error into the appellate record. Criminal defense attorneys played the game by allowing, and sometimes intentionally placing, any technical defect available into the trial record. If the defendant was later convicted, the technical error would result in a reversal of the conviction on appeal. Then, after the appellate reversal, the game resumed on retrial.

This "gamesmanship" caused both "widespread and deep" concern about the criminal justice process. Responding to these concerns, Congress passed § 269 of the Act of February 29, 1919, which provided: On the hearing of any appeal, certiorari, writ of error, or motion for a new trial, in any case, civil or criminal, the court shall give judgment after an examination of the entire record before the court, without regard to technical errors, defects, or exceptions which do not affect the substantive rights of the parties.

This law and others like it came to be known as harmless error rules.

Underlying these rules is the belief that some errors occurring during the trial process do not affect the outcome. As explained by Justice Rutledge:

The general object [of the harmless error rule] was simple: To substitute judgment for [the] automatic application of rules; to preserve review as a check upon arbitrary action and essential unfairness in trials, but at the same time to make the process perform that function without giving men fairly convicted the multiplicity of loopholes which any highly rigid and minutely detailed scheme of errors, especially in relation to procedure, will engender and reflect in a printed record. [74]

Issues which the court has stated will not fall under Harmless Error

Coerced Confessions

Denying the defendant the right to counsel

Denying the defendant the right to an impartial judge [75]

Sometimes the prosecutor "forgets' to include information in a report or fails to present a complete report to the defense. As you read above, technical errors in pleadings do not reverse decisions, and are harmless error.

These immunities differ depending upon the stage of the criminal proceeding. Although immunity is enjoyed by prosecutors, the theory of immunity was not intended to shield prosecutors from committing unscrupulous and/or criminal acts. Immunity was intended to protect against "ERRORS OF OMISSION" or harmless error, defined as unintentional errors or reasonable errors. Immunity was not intended to excuse criminal acts such as criminal conspiracy, witness tampering, obstruction of justice, bribery, extortion, perjury, presenting false evidence, presenting witnesses to give false testimony, and more.

A law enforcement officer approaches a prosecutor or a judge (if the local laws allow law enforcement to approach a judge) to get a warrant. Most times now the prosecutor wants to be the person approaching the judge because the prosecutor wants to be sure there is a possibility of having a winning case. Prosecutors did not like having law enforcement dropping cases into the lap of a prosecutor because the prosecutor usually had to clean up the mess created by rogue law enforcement. Law enforcement did not care; they would not be presenting evidence to the judge or the jury so they would drop it on the prosecutor.

The prosecutor can pick and choose which cases they want to prosecute. The acceptance of the case presented does not depend upon whether law enforcement has given enough evidence for a conviction. The prosecutor can ignore evidence against prospective defendants who are friends, sons and daughters of friends, or person who contribute to the prosecutor in other ways. The prosecutor will want all warrants to go through their office so they can control the system.

Criminal Justice is Selective Enforcement

In 1994, a lady came to me and told me she had given $10,000 to a palm-reading gypsy. The gypsy told the lady that the $10,000 was to erase a cloud over the life of the lady. I found the gypsy, did what I had to do, and enabled the client to receive $20,000 in repayment, which under SC law was termed as swindling and enabled double damages.

Soon thereafter, another victim of the same palm-reading gypsy told me that the gypsy had suckered him into buying the gypsy a car and letting her control his bank account while he was deployed as a merchant marine. The gypsy told my client that she was not married, and he was very gullible. She told him that they would get married when he returned. My client did not know that the gypsy was married, and the "brother" she identified to the client was her husband. My client allowed the "brother" to be added onto the bank account to pay bills while the client was deployed. Another victim surfaced, having given the gypsy approximately $28,000.

I investigated this gypsy family and went to a local magistrate to get a warrant. I gave my investigative report to the judge/magistrate. He told me the report was better than any he had seen from local law enforcement. The magistrate told me that the prosecutor would not allow any warrants to be issued without the permission of the prosecutor. The judge called the prosecutor on the telephone while I was sitting across the table from the magistrate. The judge told the prosecutor that I was in the office, and that I had presented sufficient and complete evidence of a crime having been committed. The judge asked for a warrant. The prosecutor refused.

The prosecutor gave no excuse other than the report did not come from law enforcement. The prosecutor knew me personally, and this became a huge political issue. With a bit of backroom work, I did get my warrant, convinced law enforcement to put the warrant into NCIC (National Criminal Information Center) database, and I traveled to another state to have the gypsy arrested. No one knew I had the warrant information in my hands or that I had given the info to the local law enforcement in the city where I had the gypsy arrested.

This had become a personal thing. Later, I was retained by other defendants in court proceedings. I had gotten the attention of the prosecutor on the first gypsy case, but the attitude of the prosecutor (and some of his staff) was that the victims of the gypsies were so stupid to believe the gypsies, and the victims deserved to be fleeced. You would not believe the back and forth between the prosecutor and me as I tried to get a warrant for what the gypsies did to the merchant marine and the lady who lost $28,000. I fought like hell, offended people in the prosecutor's office, but I got the warrant.

This is but one reason the prosecutor wants all warrants to pass through their office. It is all about winning and control and had nothing to do with the validity of the report submitted to them. They do as they please, and for their benefit. The magistrate was ready to give me the warrant, but the prosecutor "selectively" chose not to allow the warrant.

If the prosecutor approaches a judge with a warrant, the judge must sign the warrant in order for law enforcement to arrest an individual.

The reason for the warrant is not always because a person has committed a crime. A crime must be listed on the warrant, but the defendant can be arrested for menial crimes in order to harass or to extract information from the person being arrested.

The prosecutor has little concern about making mistakes or violating the rights of the defendant. You have heard "if they want you, they will get you" and believe me, they can. Just ask former Senator Ted Stevens, who died in an unfortunate airplane crash after his sentence was overturned for prosecutorial misconduct.

Errors could be the pathway to a reversal. The defendant is looking for an error that was not harmless, and one that was an act of commission (intentional).

The prosecutor will not lose their job. Law enforcement officers rarely lose their jobs if marginal information is given to the prosecutor to have a warrant issued. It is the prosecutor who is liable, but when there is no liability, no one is liable.

Will the prosecutor cry "harmless error" because they were overwhelmed, busy, human, or just forgot to do something?

This brings us to the catch phrase used by prosecutors when they get caught making trampling on the rights of a defendant; reasonable error.

Reasonable Error

Is it reasonable error to fail to give all the exculpatory evidence to the defense attorney?

Is it reasonable error to fail to notify the defense of all witnesses?

There is a difference between reasonable error and harmless error. If the prosecutor can convince a judge that the error was reasonable, then the prosecutor must prove to the judge that the error was "harmless."

Harmless error occurs when a mistake is made, such as "misplacing" exculpatory evidence and failing to give the evidence to the defense attorney.

Harmless error does not include paying a witness to give false testimony against a defendant, reducing the time of incarceration of an informant, planting a jail house snitch next to a defendant to bypass the fact that the defendant has a lawyer, or jury tampering.

In fact, these are not errors at all. These are corrupt acts performed by prosecutors as they seek a conviction. Anything found to be misconduct on the part of a prosecutor is not a mistake; it is a ploy. If the ploy is exposed, the prosecutor calls it a mistake, but there are too many people in the office to make this a "mistake." Someone in the office has to have a conscience, don't they?

Nothing is ever said. The joke is on the defendant.

THE OVERZEALOUS PROSECUTOR

An Essay from Brian Sun

Below is an excerpt from an essay written Brian A. Sun, entitled The Overzealous Prosecutor. I highly recommend this article.

"For instance, I knew a prosecutor who had a reputation for consistently withholding discovery and misleading the court about the prosecution's evidence. Even within his own office, this lawyer was reputed to be "out of control" and an embarrassment to his colleagues. Approximately three days before I was scheduled to begin a trial against this prosecutor, I learned of a tape recording with statements made by my client that had not been turned over as required under the criminal discovery rules.

Even before this incident, I had complained informally about the prosecutor's conduct to other lawyers in that prosecutor's office and to a supervisor. After learning of this tape recording, I erupted like a rocket. I obeyed the first rule of combat and calmed down first. Then, cool and collected, I protested the prosecutor's conduct vigorously to his superiors and specifically outlined the lengthy protest I intended to make to the judge. The prosecutor's office decided to dismiss the case against my client with the warning that it would re-indict the matter "after further review of the case."

Fortunately, this promised review did not occur, and my client became a beneficiary of the prosecutor's serious error in judgment".[76]

According to the case against Thompson, the prosecutor and law enforcement are only liable if there is a custom of constitutional neglect. This is what killed the allegation in the Thompson case; the word "custom" implies a regular practice. Thompson's award was thrown out because it was ruled a one-time failure to train, and there was no pattern of repeat behavior, as in "custom."

A case came up in the next year, showing the same misconduct, but Thompson's attorneys could not go back and tell the justices "...see, I told you there was a custom of misconduct." Maybe they should have waited a year or so and filed both cases together or put Thompson after Juan Smith's case.

Making the boss liable, or the person who hired the bad actor, comes under the heading of "respondeat superior" which is Latin for "let the master answer" and makes the prosecutor liable. Respondeat superior is the boss, meaning superior. The boss could be an immediate supervisor, or in theory, the municipality.

The theory of holding a municipality liable is a way of going for the deep pocket.

A municipality cannot be held liable for bad prosecutors; prosecutors are elected.

No one is liable for bad prosecutors, not even prosecutors.

RESPONSIBILITY AND ACCOUNTABILITY

The Myth

A great and easy to read article was found in the Yale Law Review, written by law students, David Keenan, Deborah Jane Cooper, David Lebowitz, and Tamar Lever, and published Tuesday, October 25, 2011. The name of the essay is:

The Myth of Prosecutorial Accountability after Connick v. Thompson: Why Existing Professional Responsibility Measures Cannot Protect Against Prosecutorial Misconduct.

Yale Law Review excerpts of essay: Myth of Prosecutorial Accountability

Below are excerpts from the article. The entire article can be found on the Yale Law Review website.

On March 29, 2011, the Supreme Court--by a vote of five to four-- overturned a $14 million jury verdict in favor of John Thompson, a Louisiana man who spent fourteen years on death row because prosecutors withheld exculpatory blood evidence from his defense attorneys.

The Connick Court, in an opinion authored by Justice Thomas, disagreed with Thompson's argument. According to Justice Thomas's majority opinion, a single Brady violation--i.e., a one-time failure to disclose "material" evidence--is insufficient to establish liability on a failure-to-train theory.

One alternative is readily apparent from the Court's Connick decision itself: state professional disciplinary procedures. In holding that district attorneys are reasonably entitled to rely on the "professional training and ethical obligations" of their subordinates, the Court noted that "[a]n attorney who violates his or her ethical obligations is subject to professional discipline, including sanctions, suspension, and disbarment."

Prior to trial, Thompson's attorneys made a motion to inspect all material evidence and scientific reports and all materials favorable to the defendant.

In reaching this conclusion, the Court determined that professional training provided an adequate safeguard against constitutional violations. Justice Thomas, writing for the majority, specifically referenced lawyers' education in law school, their completion of the bar exam, continuing education requirements, character and fitness standards, on-the-job training from more experienced attorneys, and the potential imposition of professional discipline as reasons for rejecting single instance failure-to-train liability.

Several empirical problems hamper efforts to provide an accurate assessment of prosecutorial misconduct in the United States. First, prosecutors who engage in willful misconduct presumably do not want to be discovered and therefore take steps to conceal their misdeeds. Even a scrupulous prosecutor who witnesses a colleague engage in misconduct may nevertheless fail to report it for fear of professional repercussions.

Second, prosecutors' offices enjoy considerable autonomy in shaping their internal policies. Although judicial oversight should theoretically check this autonomy, courts are generally loath to interfere with the inner workings of a coordinate branch of government.

Third, the vast majority of known instances of prosecutorial misconduct come to light only during the course of a drawn-out trial or appellate proceeding. John Thompson's ordeal is illustrative: the blood evidence that ultimately exculpated Thompson was obtained at the eleventh hour through the "chance discovery" of a lone investigator hired by his defense team. But most criminal cases in the United States result in plea bargains, which are rarely the subject of extensive investigation or judicial review, creating a heightened risk of undetected prosecutorial misconduct in the plea-bargaining context.

Finally, those in the best position to report misconduct--namely judges, other prosecutors, and defense attorneys and their clients--are often disincentivized from doing so for both strategic and political reasons. From the defendant's perspective, there is little to gain from filing a bar complaint and much to lose.

Since the nineteenth century, American courts have recognized that prosecutors are immune from tort liability for actions performed in the line of duty. After decades of general adherence to this principle by state courts, the Supreme Court recognized prosecutors' common-law tort immunity from suits for malicious prosecution in 1927, affirming per curiam a decision of the Court of Appeals for the Second Circuit which held that "[t]he immunity is absolute, and is grounded on principles of public policy."

Alternatives to civil liability have proven no more successful. In the course of upholding official immunity, the Supreme Court in Imbler wrote that prosecutorial misconduct "is reprehensible, warranting criminal prosecution as well as disbarment," rather than civil damages.

As John Thompson wrote in an op-ed published shortly after the Supreme Court's decision: "I don't care about the money. I just want to know why the prosecutors who hid evidence, sent me to prison for something I didn't do and nearly had me killed are not in jail themselves." However, criminal sanctions for prosecutors who violate Brady are exceedingly rare.

Similarly, bar discipline procedures have not proved a fruitful sanction for deterring prosecutorial misconduct. Many state bar disciplinary systems barely seem to contemplate prosecutorial misconduct as a cognizable complaint, focusing instead on fee disputes and failure to diligently pursue a client's claim. Indeed, only one of the five prosecutors responsible for violating John Thompson's constitutional rights has ever been disciplined by the attorney grievance system in place in Louisiana. Ironically, that prosecutor is Michael Riehlmann, the only one of the five who was not directly involved in prosecuting Thompson's case or implicated in any of the Brady violations that occurred and the only attorney to ever report the violations to Louisiana's Office of Disciplinary Counsel (ODC). Five years after Gerry Deegan had confessed to him about suppressing the blood evidence, Riehlmann reported his conversation with Deegan to ODC after Thompson's attorneys inquired about his knowledge of the newly discovered crime lab report. The Louisiana Attorney Discipline Board subsequently recommended that Riehlmann's law license be suspended for six months because he failed to report Deegan's confession within a "reasonable time" and this failure was "prejudicial to the administration of justice." The Supreme Court of Louisiana, however, determined that Riehlmann's behavior was "merely negligent" and that a public reprimand was the appropriate sanction.

In 1999, Chicago Tribune reporters Maurice Possley and Ken Armstrong identified 381 homicide cases nationally in which Brady violations produced conviction reversals. Not a single prosecutor in those cases was publicly sanctioned.

For over one hundred years, states have looked to the ABA for guidance when constructing their local rules for attorney discipline. The Model Rules of Professional Conduct, first promulgated in 1983 and substantially revised in 2002, have proven especially influential. Every state save California has adopted attorney ethics codes that substantially mirror the Model Rules.

The Model Rules generally do not distinguish between private attorneys and prosecutors. All lawyers are expected to conduct themselves in accordance with its general provisions. Model Rule 3.8 is exceptional, however, in that it defines certain "special" ethical duties unique to prosecutors, including the obligation not to pursue charges against an individual in the absence of probable cause and the affirmative responsibility to disclose exculpatory evidence in a timely fashion.

Rule 3.8 embodies Justice Sutherland's general admonition in Berger v. United States that

State disciplinary authorities have the potential to rein in unethical behavior by prosecutors. They can only perform this function, however, if states adopt ethics rules with biteTo date, only five states have adopted the provisions in full or modified form. Eleven other states are currently considering amending their versions of Rule 3.8. The remainder thirty-four states in total, have taken no action.

The corollary to the ethics rules are the disciplinary systems established to enforce those rules. Without consistent enforcement by the bodies charged with overseeing attorney discipline, ethics rules are little more than empty promises.

Many states actively discourage potential grievance filers by erecting procedural barriers like statutes of limitations, notarized document requirements, or mandatory referral programs. Moreover, disciplinary agencies rarely initiate investigations sua sponte, preferring instead to rely on those personally affected by lawyer misconduct to bring claims to the agency's attention.

Mississippi's bar association, for instance, goes to great lengths to warn complainants of the serious consequences that can result from filing a complaint. The bar association's website begins its appeal by reminding potential filers that "lawyers are human."

Measuring state disciplinary systems' responsiveness to prosecutorial misconduct in particular is hampered by a paucity of available statistics. Only one state, Illinois, publishes data on the number of complaints of prosecutorial misconduct received and investigated on an annual basis. But if that data are indicative of the way most states handle such claims, they paint a bleak picture. The statistics show that, in 2010, charges against 4016 attorneys were docketed by the Illinois Attorney Registration and Disciplinary Commission, of which ninety-nine involved charges of prosecutorial misconduct. Only one of these ninety-nine cases, however, actually reached a formal hearing. In other words, the Illinois disciplinary commission held as many formal hearings involving charges of prosecutorial misconduct as it did charges of "bad faith avoidance of a student loan."[77]

In an abstract placed on a reprint of the same essay above, the authors made the following statement:

Our study demonstrates that professional responsibility measures as they are currently composed do a poor job of policing prosecutorial misconduct.

However, we also take seriously the Supreme Court's insistence that those measures should function as the primary means of deterring misconduct. Accordingly, in addition to noting the deficiencies of professional responsibility measures, we offer a series of recommendations for enhancing their effectiveness.[78]

PROSECUTOR KNOWINGLY PRESENTS FAULTY LAB RESULTS

A Notable Dissent

Chief Judge Alex Kozinski gives a stinging dissent about a Brady Motion violation, and the fact that courts ignore these violations.

Let me set up the case:

Kenneth Olsen was convicted of developing a biological agent, identified as ricin, and was planning to use it as a weapon. Olsen claimed he was curious about weird things and was not going to use it as a weapon.

Washington State Police took some allergy pills from Olsen and sent the pills to a state lab. The forensic scientist examining the pills was Arnold Melnikoff. Melnikoff's lab was not set up to test for ricin, so Melnikoff dumped out the pills onto a piece of paper which was in the same area that ricin had been tested, thus contaminating the pills. The FBI said the pills were contaminated with ricin.

Melnikoff had run the Montana State Crime Laboratory. The State of Washington did a background check on Melnikoff and found there were issues involving misconduct in his case work, which carried over into courtroom testimony. Also, flaws in Melnikoff's work resulted in at least 3 inmates being exonerated. ("Inmates" being exonerated, of course, means the persons who were exonerated were found guilty based upon the tainted evidence.)

Melnikoff was fired from the Washington State Police.

Even though Olsen's lawyer knew that Melnikoff was being investigated, a federal prosecutor lied about the nature of the investigation, and the fact that Melnikoff probably contaminated the allergy pills.

Federal prosecutors withheld evidence about the contaminated pills and the nature of the investigation of Melnikoff. No intended victims were identified because there were none. The case seemed to be ready to be overturned.

The court ruled that the pill issue was no big deal, and the conviction was upheld against Olsen. Chief Judge Kozinski issued his dissent and made the following comments.

Judge Alex Kozinski on Kenneth Olsen

There is an epidemic of Brady violations abroad in the land. Only judges can put a stop to it.

I wish I could say that the prosecutor's unprofessionalism here is the exception, that his propensity for shortcuts and indifference to his ethical and legal responsibilities is a rare blemish and source of embarrassment to an otherwise diligent and scrupulous corps of attorneys staffing prosecutors' offices across the country. But it wouldn't be true. Brady violations have reached epidemic proportions in recent years, and the federal and state reporters bear testament to this unsettling trend.

When a public official behaves with such casual disregard for his constitutional obligations and the rights of the accused, it erodes the public's trust in our justice system, and chips away at the foundational premises of the rule of law. When such transgressions are acknowledged yet forgiven by the courts, we endorse and invite their repetition.

Due to the nature of a Brady violation, it's highly unlikely wrongdoing will ever come to light in the first place. This creates a serious moral hazard for those prosecutors who are more interested in winning a conviction than serving justice.

In the rare event that the suppressed evidence does surface, the consequences usually leave the prosecution no worse than had it complied with Brady from the outset.

Professional discipline is rare, and violations seldom give rise to liability for money damages. Criminal liability for causing an innocent man to lose decades of his life behind bars is practically unheard of. If the violation is found to be material (a standard that will almost never be met under the panel's construction), the prosecution gets a do-over, making it no worse off than if it had disclosed the evidence in the first place. [79]

But the biggest problem is that new evidence is hard--and often impossible--to find. If it's a physical crime, police secure the crime scene and seize anything that looks like it could be relevant. The chance of going back years later and picking up new clues is vanishingly small. The trick then is to get whatever evidence the police have, assuming they didn't destroy it or release it once it was clear that it wouldn't be used at trial. If the crime is non-physical, such as fraud, child pornography or computer hacking, the police seize all the relevant computers, hard drives and paper records (including any exculpatory evidence the suspect may have there) and may well discard them after the conviction becomes final.

I think it's fair to assume--though there is no way of knowing--that the number of exculpations in recent years understates the actual number of innocent prisoners by an order, and probably two orders, of magnitude. [80]

Buckley: Corrupt Prosecutor and Expert

As you see from the footnote above, there is a reference to a case noted as Buckley 509 US at 268. I wanted to see the case in the reference, and you and I both will be glad I did.

This case went before the US Supreme Court, and the opinion was delivered by Justice John Paul Stevens.

Petitioner Buckley sought damages, under 42 U. S. C. § 1983, from respondent prosecutors for fabricating evidence during the preliminary investigation of a highly publicized rape and murder in Illinois and making false statements at a press conference announcing the return of an indictment against him. He claimed that when three separate lab studies failed to make a reliable connection between a boot print at the murder site and his boots, respondents obtained a positive identification from one Robbins, who allegedly was known for her willingness to fabricate unreliable expert testimony. Thereafter, they convened a grand jury for the sole purpose of investigating the murder, and 10 months later, respondent Fitzsimmons, the State's Attorney, announced the indictment at the news conference. [81]

As the case comes to us, we have no occasion to consider whether some or all of respondents' conduct may be protected by qualified immunity. Moreover, we make two important assumptions about the case: first, that petitioner's allegations are entirely true; and, second, that they allege constitutional violations for which § 1983 provides a remedy. Our statement of facts is therefore derived entirely from petitioner's complaint and is limited to matters relevant to respondents' claim to absolute immunity. [82]

Funny that the judge John Paul Stevens said he believed the petitioner, not the respondent, the prosecutors. You would think the opposing side in the matter would dispute facts, but the court believed everything presented on behalf of the defendant. That had to be quite a slap in the face to the prosecutor, or the attorney who had to represent the prosecutor before the Supreme Court.

Realistically, the prosecutors probably laughed at this comment. While I find it funny, the prosecutors knew that appearing before the Supreme Court was a hoop jump and they really do not care what the justices said if they lose the case. It was an "oh, well" moment for the prosecutors.

Some of the misconduct committed by prosecutors is so commonplace that it is no surprise that they have cases overturned. Prosecutors and law enforcement know that by the time any case is overturned, they have flexed their muscles and proved they can arrest and prosecute who they want, and even if it is overturned, they have made their statement to the public, that they can do what they want, when they want, punish you, and ruin your life if you "mess with us."

Thereafter, having failed to obtain sufficient evidence to support petitioner's (or anyone else's) arrest, respondents convened a special grand jury for the sole purpose of investigating the Nicarico case. After an 8 month investigation, during which the grand jury heard the testimony of over 100 witnesses, including the bootprint experts, it was still unable to return an indictment. On January 27, 1984, respondent Fitzsimmons admitted in a public statement that there was insufficient evidence to indict anyone for the rape and murder of Jeanine Nicarico. Although no additional evidence was obtained in the interim, the indictment was returned in March, when Fitzsimmons held the defamatory press conference so shortly before the primary election. Petitioner was then arrested, and because he was unable to meet the bond (set at $3 million), he was held in jail. [83]*

Buckley was arrested and, unable to meet the bond, held in jail. Robbins provided the principal evidence against him at trial, but the jury was unable to reach a verdict. When Robbins died before Buckley's retrial, all charges were dropped and he was released after three years of incarceration. In the § 1983 action, the District Court held that respondents were entitled to absolute immunity for the fabricated evidence claim but not for the press conference claim. However, the Court of Appeals ruled that they had absolute immunity on both claims, theorizing that prosecutors are entitled to absolute immunity when out-of-court acts cause injury only to the extent a case proceeds in court, but are entitled only to qualified immunity if the constitutional wrong is complete before the case begins. On remand from this Court, it found that nothing in Burns v.Reed,500 U. S. 478-in which the Court held that prosecutors had absolute immunity for their actions in participating in a probable-cause hearing but not in giving advice to the police-undermined its initial holding. [84]

We first address petitioner's argument that the prosecutors are not entitled to absolute immunity for the claim that they conspired to manufacture false evidence that would link his boot with the boot print the murderer left on the front door. To obtain this false evidence, petitioner submits, the prosecutors shopped for experts until they found one who would provide the opinion they sought. App. 7-9. At the time of this witness shopping the assistant prosecutors were working hand in hand with the sheriff's detectives under the joint supervision of the sheriff and state's attorney Fitzsimmons.

It was well after the alleged fabrication of false evidence concerning the boot print that a special grand jury was impaneled. And when it finally was convened, its immediate purpose was to conduct a more thorough investigation of the crime--not to return an indictment against a suspect whom there was already probable cause to arrest. Buckley was not arrested, in fact, until 10 months after the grand jury had been convened and had finally indicted him. Under these circumstances, the prosecutors' conduct occurred well before they could properly claim to be acting as advocates. [85]

The bottom line was that the prosecutor and the law enforcement obtained "forensic" evidence from a person they knew would say whatever they needed said, basically to lie for the prosecutor in court. The forensic person was known to be questionable in character and expertise, but they got her report to the grand jury.

This was in the investigative stage, before the indictment; this was not covered by absolute immunity. The prosecutor and the law enforcement railroaded this guy.

I wonder what would have happened if the forensic lady, Robbins, had not died before the retrial, and the charges being dropped.

There is the problem; proving a prosecutor violated "qualified immunity" because he violated a law which "reasonable" prosecutor would have known. Is it a defense for a prosecutor to state that he "did not know "what he was doing was a violation of a law?" That is a weak argument for challenging a charge of misconduct during the investigative stage of the case, which is the only time qualified immunity is applied.

A prosecutor and law enforcement (they have to work together in order to get a warrant or have a grand jury hand down and indictment) get together and use information they know is wrong and fabricated, but have a good shot at a plea or conviction at trial, and the warrant is issued.

Why not? Who is going to care?

THE CRIME OF SUBORNING PERJURY BY A PROSECUTOR

The Prosecution Conspiracy Team

If a prosecutor and law enforcement conspire to have a jail house informant give false testimony, I assume it depends upon the timeframe of the solicitation of the false testimony to determine if the prosecutor has absolute immunity. Even the solicitation of false testimony, which is basically asking a person to lie, is a crime of suborning perjury. The act of asking a person to lie, regardless whether the person makes it to court to testify, is a crime. The person does not need to testify for the crime to have been committed. All that has to happen is for law enforcement or a prosecutor to ask a person to lie, and the crime is committed. If the person refuses to testify, or changes his mind, or is not used as a witness, it is still a crime. This crime can also be applied to a private citizen, and you know if a defendant or defendant's attorney asked a person to lie, it will be big trouble.

If a jail-house informant is going to submit testimony, false or not, the testimony will initially be in affidavit form so the informant cannot back out or change his testimony. Of course, this testimony has a price, and the inmate wants to make sure he gets the deal he was promised.

A law enforcement officer wanted to arrest my client. He filled out the warrant and presented it to a judge to be signed. The law enforcement officer did not present this warrant to a prosecutor. The judge questioned the warrant.

The law enforcement officer told the judge not to worry about the accuracy of the warrant because the plan was to make the defendant take a plea, and "this will never to go court." Using that fabricated warrant in court would be covered by absolute immunity for the prosecutor, even after misconduct in the investigative stage. The charges were dropped after I made quite a bit of noise, and the misconduct of the prosecutor was never addressed, nor was the fact that the law enforcement officer falsified the information on the warrant.

If the law enforcement officer told the prosecutor that false information was being presented to the magistrate and the prosecutor took the case to the trial, knowing that some material information on the warrant was incorrect, you would think the prosecutor would be liable. The prosecutor will claim absolute immunity, and no accountability will be suffered by the prosecutor.

A prosecutor needs no immunity if he is honest, but the theory of immunity is that the prosecutor can't do his job if he must look over his shoulder every minute, wondering if his aggressive prosecution has strayed over into misconduct.

Specifically, under a qualified immunity regime, the victim of misconduct can only maintain an action by defeating the criminal charges and proving that the prosecutor violated clearly established constitutional law with a culpable state of mind. [86]

LACK OF ACCOUNTABILITY BY THE PROSECUTOR

Center for Public Integrity

Specifically, in 2003 the Center for Public Integrity reported its finding that since 1970 there have been over 2000 cases in which prosecutorial misconduct by state and local prosecutors was sufficiently prejudicial to require charges to be dismissed, convictions to be reversed, or sentences to be reduced. In 513 additional cases, prosecutorial misconduct was discussed in dissenting and concurring opinions. And in thousands of other cases, appellate courts found prosecutorial misconduct but upheld the convictions under the harmless error standard. The report catalogued fifty-four cases of prosecutorial misconduct in which innocent people were convicted of serious crimes including murder, rape, kidnapping, and robbery; in many of these cases, the innocent were sentenced to death. Yet, of the 2000 cases of prejudicial prosecutorial misconduct, prosecutors were disciplined in only forty-four cases and were never criminally prosecuted. [87]

Of those 2000 cases of prosecutorial misconduct, there were forty-four instances of disciplinary action, and two disbarments.

Where is the risk to be an unethical prosecutor? Remember, you cannot have an unethical prosecutor without having unethical law enforcement involvement.

Even when the appellate court reverses a conviction on grounds of prosecutorial misconduct, the prosecutor who engaged in the misconduct generally, escapes any repercussions. The consequence of a reversal is that the defendant will be retried or have a new sentencing hearing. The offending prosecutor is rarely identified by name. Moreover, the loss on appeal is charged not to the original local prosecutor who committed the misconduct, but to the unfortunate lawyer in the state attorney general's office who inherited the case for purposes of the appeal. Thus, the trial attorney who engaged in the misconduct often escapes responsibility.[88]

Bodensteiner and Johns

Ivan Bodensteiner, law professor at Valparasio University, published an essay entitled "Congress Needs to Repair the Court's Damage to Section 1983" in the fall of 2010. Excerpts from this essay and comments will be found in this book.

Margaret Z. Johns, a senior lecturer at University of California, Davis, School of Law, has written extensively on this subject in journals and in briefs to the Supreme Court of the United States.

The Supreme Court granted certiorari to consider the "important and recurring issue of prosecutorial liability" under § 1983 of the Civil Rights Act of 1871.85. The Court acknowledged at the outset that § 1983, the statutory remedy for the deprivation of constitutional rights caused by an official's abuse of power, contains no immunities for prosecutors. The Supreme Court assumed, however, that Congress did not intend to abrogate all of the immunities that existed at common law, and the Court identified those immunities that were available for certain parties at common law. [89]

In an essay published in the Texas Journal on Civil Liberties and Civil Rights by Professor Ivan Bodensteiner, it was stated that qualified immunity, as described in a case Mitchell v. Forsyth, *"...[i]s an immunity from suit rather than a mere defense to liability."* [90]

In Monet v. DSS, the municipality was made liable if the employee acted as a result of policy or custom.

No government agency is going to have a "policy" of abusing a person "under the color of authority." A custom of abuse might occur, which is being used with respect to minorities filing federal lawsuits against police departments, and the municipality where the police department operates.

Sue the Municipality, Not the Employee

Bodensteiner boiled down the three reasons for going after the municipality rather than the individual law enforcement agent:

- The municipality is the policy maker.
- The municipality has the deep pockets (that is where the money is).
- Any change in behavior that deviates from policy, being tolerated, allows abuse.

Prosecutors are not accountable for misconduct, even if the misconduct is noted by the Court. As I have mentioned, trial prosecutors are rarely named in appellate briefs and/or opinions, but LA Times Harvey Weinstein, a law professor at University of California Irvine, has written two articles for the LA Times which you need to see.

First, here is a brief bio of Professor Weinstein:

Professor Weinstein has worked for the Los Angeles Times, New York Times, San Francisco Examiner and Wall Street Journal and has written more than 3,000 stories, reporting on the ground in 36 states plus the District of Columbia and Canada. He also has written about events and issues in other countries, and for a variety of publications, including California Lawyer, Juris Doctor, The Nation, New Times, the Saturday Review of Education and the Saturday Review of Science. [91]

Harvey Weinstein: The Outcry to Name Prosecutors

On October 4, 1993, Harvey Weinstein wrote a piece for the LA Times, entitled:

"U.S. Attorney Asks Court to Erase Criticism : Rulings: Appeals judges are urged to take back harsh words they had for a prosecutor who made untrue statements to a jury. Two drug convictions were overturned in the case." [92]

A lawyer/prosecutor lied to a jury, and the prosecutor wanted the judge to tone down the criticism. Is this the height of arrogance, or another example of incest within the family? Below are excerpts from Harvey Weinstein's article, October 4, 1993:

The U.S. attorney's office in Los Angeles has taken the highly unusual step of asking a federal appeals court to erase or at least soften a stingingly critical decision that accuses a prosecutor of a major ethical violation in a drug case.

That ruling reversed the convictions of two people for selling $100,000 worth of heroin to an undercover drug enforcement agent.

In a unanimous decision by three conservative judges, the appeals court said the guilty verdicts had been tainted by Assistant U.S. Atty. Jeffrey S. Sinek's "misstatements" to the jury, which denied the defendants due process of law. The opinion also said that his superiors seemed to have condoned his misconduct.

At a critical moment during the 1991 trial, a defense lawyer tried to persuade jurors that because a key player in the drug deal-- Krikor Nourian--had not testified, they could infer that his testimony would damage the government's case.

Prosecutor Sinek retorted that jurors should make no such inference. Sinek declared that although Nourian had been arrested, he had a constitutional right to remain silent and that the government could not force him to talk. That was untrue.

In reality, Nourian had given up that right. He had entered into a cooperation agreement with federal officials, promising to testify if the government requested it--a fact that did not become public until Judge Kozinski forced Sinek to admit it during the appeals hearing a year later.

Bowers responded last month with a contritely written brief attempting to persuade the appeals court judges to remove that opinion from federal court records, or to at least modify it. The U.S. attorney said neither Sinek nor the office acted with bad motives, and that errors in the case "were the unfortunate result of errors of judgment, driven, in Mr. Sinek's case, by his failure to fully understand the unique and special obligations of prosecutors."

Judicial criticism of the type leveled in this case is rare, according to legal experts.

Because of a well-established Supreme Court decision, Sinek had an obligation to disclose that Nourian had a cooperation agreement with the government. Jurors could have inferred from his failure to testify that Nourian had information that would have undercut the government's case.[93]

The prosecutor, Jeffrey S. Sinek, lied to the jury. The witness that he said had not wanted to talk and had invoked his 5th Amendment Right to remain silent, had made a deal with the prosecutor, and the prosecutor tried to hide this from the defense. The justices come down hard on Sinek. Sinek's boss, Bowers, writes a brief to the justices, asking them to remove the opinion from the federal record because Sinek had no "bad motives" and Sinek did not understand *"the unique and special obligations of prosecutors."* [94]

Senik got caught, plain and simple. Sinek passed the Bar exam for the State of California. He knew his obligations. He knew he was lying. Bowers and others in that office knew what Senik was going to do because he probably either discussed the matter or practiced some of his arguments on other lawyers in the Court. Federal investigators (probably FBI or DEA) knew the truth.

My first reaction to reading this was rage, then the story got better, and my rage tuned to shock.

A month later, on November 4, 1993, Henry Weinstein wrote another article about this case. The title of the article was:

"Court Will Not Name Reprimanded Prosecutor: Justice: Appeals judges say misstatements to jury tainted a drug case. The ruling is sharply critical of the U.S. attorney's office, but it will not single out the offender."

In response to a plea from U.S. Atty. Terree A. Bowers, a federal appeals court has removed the name of a young prosecutor from a decision accusing him of a major ethical violation in a drug case.

But the U.S. 9th Circuit Court of Appeals rejected the government's request to soften language in the ruling, which criticized the U.S. attorney's office so severely that the case has been reviewed by Atty. Gen. Janet Reno.

"The prosecutor's job isn't just to win, but to win fairly, staying well within the rules," wrote Judge Alex Kozinski in an Aug. 4 decision that reversed the convictions of two people for selling $100,000 worth of heroin to an undercover drug enforcement agent.

"The government here has strayed from this responsibility," Kozinski added.

In September, Bowers asked the appeals court to erase, or at least soften, some of the most stinging criticism. But that plea was spurned by Kozinski and two other conservative judges.

However, the judges removed the prosecutor's name after Bowers'
contended in a brief that it would do "irreparable harm" to the
prosecutor's career to identify him.

Bowers issued a statement that he appreciated "the
depersonalization of the circuit's opinion," which deleted his name
as well as that of the prosecutor. But he continued to maintain that
there had been "an unfortunate misunderstanding as to what
occurred during the trial."

He also said, "it was unfair" for the appeals court to draw broad
conclusions about the office's supervisory structure and ethical
standards because of one incident. [95]

Do you think a reprimand caused harm to the career of the dirty
prosecutor?

How many people in the prosecutor's office knew about the
misconduct before allowing the misconduct to be exposed in court?

The plea was to make the ruling "depersonalized." If I am not
mistaken, the name of the defendant is all over the pleadings, which
"personalizes" the matter. It is only fair that the prosecutor be
named.

Why would it be unfair to "draw conclusions about supervisory
structure", meaning the bosses of the dirty prosecutor? The bosses
are responsible, and the bosses gave this dirty prosecutor thegreen
light to see if he could make the charges stick.

The bosses were dirty., too.

THE JOINT EFFORT

The Prosecutor Agenda

The prosecutor creates his case before the suspect (defendant) is arrested. Law enforcement will consult with the prosecutor from the beginning to let them know the cases which law enforcement is investigating. The prosecutor will look at the information at hand and determine what information will be published on the warrant, or what information will be presented to the grand jury.

Remember: the prosecutor is there to prosecute and get a conviction. The truth is not the goal.

Many of the persons on the prosecution team know about the evidence in the file which is brought over by law enforcement. These team members are well schooled, intelligent, and resourceful people. They want to win, they have to win, and winning makes them look good to the voting public. The excuse of oversight is an outright lie, and if a prosecutor claims "oversight" as an excuse for a mistake, the prosecutor committed perjury. There is no oversight when there are many people involved in the case.

The prosecutor will have the exculpatory evidence (which is the information to be given to defense attorney after being served with the Brady Motion) which points toward the innocence of the defendant and might point toward the guilt of another person. Unless the defense knows what is in the file and can present a witness to the existence of that hidden information, the prosecution will never offer the exonerating information to the defense because the prosecutor thinks the defense will never know of the cover up.

Remember in Cone v Bell? The prosecutor hid the statement made by Cone's mother, who referred to Cone's drug habit after returning from Vietnam, enabling the prosecutor to commit perjury and paint Cone as a drug dealer.

When the prosecutor is caught hiding documents, he cries that he forgot to produce the document, it was an oversight, or it was harmless error. Law enforcement officers who worked on the case, and were probably in the courtroom during the trial, knew the prosecutor was lying.

If the defense is aware of "specific "documents in the prosecutor file which exonerates the defendant, a motion can be made to the court (directed to the judge) to make the prosecutor reveal the exact hidden information.

A good PI can make law enforcement a bit nervous or enrage them to the point of vengeance against the PI. I have enraged law enforcement (and prosecutors), and have experienced their vengeance, and I apologize to no one.

Some private investigators are more loyal to the defense attorney than to the defendant. The defendant is being held hostage by the defense attorney telling him "I am here to help you" when, at the same time, the investigator is being told by the defense attorney how to conduct the defense investigation instead of the investigator taking charge of finding the truth. The defense attorney and the PI can work together, but you never want the defense attorney restraining the PI as the PI attempts to free the defendant.

Information in the file begins with documents submitted by law enforcement. If there are statements or other evidence implicating someone other than the defendant, these pieces of evidence will never see the light of day unless the PI knows the information is in the file. The game plan proceeds. The 'trick play" is the illegal and unethical hiding of evidence which is favorable to the defense. If caught hiding the evidence, the prosecution team does not get penalized, but the defense gets to see the new evidence.

There is no oversight. Many people read, review, plan, and create documents for the prosecution. Part of the plan is to hide evidence, and if caught, apologize to the Court (heartfelt I am sure) and the Court will order the prosecutor to correct their "mistake."

Errors of Omission

The two "errors" committed by prosecutors are accidental errors (omission) and intentional errors (commission). It is almost impossible to have an accidental error because too many people are involved in the crafting of a cease for a prosecution. Many times, more than one prosecutor will be sitting at the prosecutor table in the courtroom, and all persons at the table help craft the prosecution.

If prosecutors are caught telling a lie, leaving out evidence, or any other act of misconduct, the prosecutor will cry that this act was an honest mistake, thus the behavior was an error of omission.

The only time the prosecutor raises the flag of an error, which is never really an error, is when the prosecutor is caught.

Hiding Defendant Cooperation from the Court

The threat of being charged with a little-known crime of "misprison of a felony" could be used by a prosecutor. This crime is defined as knowing that a felony was committed and the person not running to the police to tell what they know. It sounds silly, but sometimes it is used, but hardly ever will a person be convicted of this crime. These threats by a prosecutor are hidden from the Court.

One part of dealing with plea agreements is that a defendant would want the plea agreement not to reflect that the defendant cooperated with authorities, only that he agreed to certain charges to be convicted of fewer charges. The defendant does not want to go out on the street and have his friends think he became an informant in order to get out.

Look at it this way: each defendant is a candidate to become an informant, so each person who has ever been a defendant could have been an informant. Does that mean that all persons in a neighborhood who have a record (meaning most persons in low income ethnic areas) might have snitched? They probably have and are still doing it.

"A typical cooperation agreement requires the defendant to waive the presence of counsel for conversations with the handling agent."[96]

Around 1986, a former employee of a state prosecutor office became an acquaintance of mine This person was quite a character, a rough guy, but funny as hell to be around. I was working on a case involving a legislator and his drug use, and this friend of mine gave me a sheet of paper, having information printed and official, of cases from the prosecutor office which the legislator had been assigned. At least a dozen of the cases was labeled "nolle prossed," there was going to be no prosecution, all charges were dropped.

All cases were drug cases. My informant friend told me that this is where the legislator got his drugs: he drops charges against a drug dealer, and the prosecutor becomes a customer, and the prosecutor gets his stuff for free.

Failure to prosecute drug dealers, and some other criminals, will aid the prosecutor when he goes into private practice. The deal is to get the charges dropped or reduced dramatically, and all the defendant's friends will become customers. The Court, and most times the defense attorney, will not know the full reason that charges were being dropped.

As with the druggie legislator, people who run for public office promote their time as a prosecutor to show the voting public that they are protecting the public from the bad people and need to carry that protective ethic to political office. The only talent the dirty prosecutor takes into politics is the ability to use leverage against a person to get deals done on behalf of someone who is going to line his pocket with money.

After a bench warrant is issued, the prosecutor controls whether the warrant is put into NCIC, which is the National Crime Information Center database. This affects whether other jurisdictions will know of the warrant, and whether the prosecutor will pay for extradition from another area. The NCIC matter affects the bail bondsman more than it does any other part of the criminal justice family, other than giving the defendant a free pass. I will discuss the issue of the NCIC in the section of the bail bondsman. This is another way the prosecutor can do favors for defendants and benefit from these favors when the prosecutor leaves and goes into private practice. This is no act of omission. Law enforcement knows if the warrant is in NCIC, and the joint effort continues.

REASONS TO WORRY ABOUT OUR CRIMINAL JUSTICE SYSTEM

Eugene Volokh

Eugene Volokh, who clerked for Judge Alex Kozinski, and has taught law courses at UCLA, wrote an article for the Washington Post which was published July 14, 2005, entitled "12 Reasons to Worry About our Criminal Justice System, From a Prominent Conservative Federal Judge."

Below are excerpts from the twelve reasons, put forth by Eugene Volokh, as interpreted from Judge Alex Kozinski:

1. Eyewitnesses are highly reliable.

This belief is so much part of our culture that one often hears talk of a "mere" circumstantial case as contrasted to a solid case based on eyewitness testimony. In fact, research shows that eyewitness identifications are highly unreliable, especially where the witness and the perpetrator are of different races. Eyewitness reliability is further compromised when the identification occurs under the stress of a violent crime, an accident or catastrophic event -- which pretty much covers all situations where identity is in dispute at trial. In fact, mistaken eyewitness testimony was a factor in more than a third of wrongful conviction cases.

2. Fingerprint evidence is foolproof.

Not so. Identifying prints that are taken by police using fingerprinting equipment and proper technique may be a relatively simple process, but latent prints left in the field are often smudged and incomplete, and the identification process becomes more art than science

Perhaps the best-known example of such an error occurred in 2004 when the FBI announced that a latent print found on a plastic bag near a Madrid terrorist bombing was "a 100 percent match" to Oregon attorney Brandon Mayfield. The FBI eventually conceded error when Spanish investigators linked the print to someone else.

3. Other types of forensic evidence are scientifically proven and therefore infallible.

With the exception of DNA evidence (which has its own issues), what goes for fingerprints goes double and triple for other types of forensic evidence: "Spectrographic voice identification error rates are as high as 63%, depending on the type of voice sample tested. Handwriting error rates average around 40% and sometimes approach 100%. False-positive error rates for bite marks run as high as 64%. Those for microscopic hair comparisons are about 12% (using results of mitochondrial DNA testing as the criterion)."

Some fields of forensic expertise are built on nothing but guesswork and false common sense. Many defendants have been convicted and spent countless years in prison based on evidence by arson experts who were later shown to be little better than witch doctors. Cameron Todd Willingham may have lost his life over it.

4. DNA evidence is infallible.

This is true to a point. DNA comparison, when properly conducted by an honest, trained professional will invariably reach the correct result. But the integrity of the result depends on a variety of factors that are, unfortunately, not nearly so foolproof: the evidence must be gathered and preserved so as to avoid contamination; the testing itself must be conducted so that the two samples being compared do not contaminate each other; the examiner must be competent and honest. As numerous scandals involving DNA testing labs have shown, these conditions cannot be taken for granted, and DNA evidence is only as good as the weakest link in the chain.

5. Human memories are reliable.

Science now tells us that this view of human memory is fundamentally flawed. The mind not only distorts and embellishes memories, but a variety of external factors can affect how memories are retrieved and described

6. Confessions are infallible because innocent people never confess.

We now know that this is not true. Innocent people do confess with surprising regularity. Harsh interrogation tactics, a variant of Stockholm syndrome, the desire to end the ordeal, emotional and financial exhaustion, family considerations and the youth or feeble-mindedness of the suspect can result in remarkably detailed confessions that are later shown to be utterly false.

7. Juries follow instructions.

This is a presumption -- actually more of a guess -- that we've elevated to a rule of law. It is, of course, necessary that we do so because it links the jury's fact-finding process to the law. In fact, however, we know very little about what juries actually do when they decide cases. Do they consider the instructions at all? Do they consider all of the instructions or focus on only some? Do they understand the instructions or are they confused?

8. Prosecutors play fair.

The Supreme Court has told us in no uncertain terms that a prosecutor's duty is to do justice, not merely to obtain a conviction. It has also laid down some specific rules about how prosecutors, and the people who work for them, must behave -- principal among them that the prosecution turn over to the defense exculpatory evidence in the possession of the prosecution and the police.

Beyond that, we have what I have described elsewhere as an "epidemic of Brady violations abroad in the land," a phrase that has caused much controversy but brought about little change in the way prosecutors operate in the United States.

9. The prosecution is at a substantial disadvantage because it must prove its case beyond a reasonable doubt.

Juries are routinely instructed that the defendant is presumed innocent and the prosecution must prove guilt beyond a reasonable doubt, but we don't really know whether either of these instructions has an effect on the average juror. Nor do we know whether juries really draw a distinction between proof by a preponderance, proof by clear and convincing evidence and proof beyond a reasonable doubt. Even more troubling are doubts raised by psychological research showing that "whoever makes the first assertion about something has a large advantage over everyone who denies it later." The tendency is more pronounced for older people than for younger ones, and increases the longer the time-lapse between assertion and denial. So is it better to stand mute rather than deny an accusation? Apparently not, because "when accusations or assertions are met with silence, they are more likely to feel true."

10. Police are objective in their investigations.

In many ways, this is the bedrock assumption of our criminal justice process. Police investigators have vast discretion about what leads to pursue, which witnesses to interview, what forensic tests to conduct and countless other aspects of the investigation. Police also have a unique opportunity to manufacture or destroy evidence, influence witnesses, extract confessions and otherwise direct the investigation so as to stack the deck against people they believe should be convicted.

11. Guilty pleas are conclusive proof of guilt.

Many people, including judges, take comfort in knowing that an overwhelming number of criminal cases are resolved by guilty plea rather than trial. Whatever imperfections there may be in the trial and criminal charging process, they believe, are washed away by the fact that the defendant ultimately consents to a conviction. But this fails to take into account the trend of bringing multiple counts for a single incident -- thereby vastly increasing the risk of a life-shattering sentence in case of conviction -- as well as the creativity of prosecutors in hatching up criminal cases where no crime exists and the overcriminalization of virtually every aspect of American life.

It also ignores that many defendants cannot, as a practical matter, tell their side of the story at trial because they fear being impeached with prior convictions or other misconduct. And, of course, if the trial process is perceived as highly uncertain, or even stacked in favor of the prosecution, the incentive to plead guilty to some charge that will allow the defendant to salvage a portion of his life, becomes immense. If the prosecution offers a take-it-or-leave-it plea bargain before disclosing exculpatory evidence, the defendant may cave to the pressure, throwing away a good chance of an acquittal.

12. Long sentences deter crime.[97]

Comments on "reasons to worry"

As a humble layman, having not been a lawyer or a judge, I will disagree with the last of the twelve reasons. Even though it costs a lot of money to keep these criminals in prison, crime rates are decreasing in most area (probably except for Chicago and Baltimore).

A scary thing that a prosecutor can do is to be guilty of prosecutorial misconduct which allows a guilty defendant to go free. Could the ego of a cocky prosecutor think their misconduct might come out at

trial and let a dangerous person go free, just because of laziness, not producing Brady material, or even sabotaging a case?

I found a great website which shows exonerations in the United States. *According to the National Registry of Exonerations, there have been 1,740 exonerations in the United States since 1989.*[98]

If a person divided out the years since 1989, the annual number would not seem very many. The things to consider are the time served by the innocent person before being exonerated (which takes years after a conviction), and the fact that the figure of 1,740 is probably a lot fewer than the ones who were convicted by misconduct by prosecutors and law enforcement.

MARGARET Z. JOHNSON PROSECUTORIAL IMMUNITY

Absolute prosecutorial immunity

Below is the concluding statement made by Margaret Z. John in her article Reconsidering Absolute Prosecutorial Immunity:

Absolute prosecutorial immunity should be reconsidered. Empirical studies establish that prosecutorial misconduct is a significant factor leading to the wrongful conviction of many innocent people. The supposed checks on prosecutorial misconduct fail to deter or punish misconduct or to protect the wrongfully accused. Civil liability will provide a needed check on misconduct and a needed remedy to the victim. Qualified immunity provides sufficient protection to the honest prosecutor while permitting the development of constitutional doctrine, the evolution of enforceable professional norms, and the implementation of needed remedies. Ultimately, prosecutorial accountability for constitutional misconduct will enhance the integrity of the criminal justice system. [99]

Being in the courtroom and watching the unethical prosecutor, the unethical law enforcement, the knowing and sometimes helpless (or not really caring) defense attorney, the victimized defendant, and the happy bail bondsman, is like watching a playground game of football in my old neighborhood. The big boys always controlled the game.

THE BAIL BONDSMAN

Bye, Bye Civil Rights

"Screw immunity, you signed your life away, your civil rights are gone. I will come into your house, no warrant, and get you." So, says the bail bondsman, and I was a bail bondsman as well as a private investigator. That is what we did.

The bail bondsman is the most dependent member of the criminal justice family. The power that the bondsman has is he has to make sure the defendant appears in court at the appointed time. No family member actively courts favor with the bail bondsman, but pressure is placed upon the bondsman by the other family members

Not All States Allow Private Bail Bond Agents

The following states do not allow a private bail bond process:

Massachusetts, Maine, Oregon, Illinois, Kentucky, Nebraska, Wisconsin, and Washington, D.C.

While I traveled to many states in southeastern United States to apprehend fugitives, and to NY, my experience comes from my being licensed in South Carolina and communicating with bondsmen in states which allowed private bail bondsmen.

As you will read later, use of private bondsmen is a money-making vehicle for the prosecutor's office and the municipality. I can only assume that if a person becomes a fugitive, the court will hold the maker of the bond liable and enforce the payment through a lawsuit. When a private bonding company is used, the bonding company is liable to the court for the face amount of the bond, and the bond company has to collect the bond amount from the maker of the bond. Therefore, it is easier and a more expedient to have a bond paid by a bond company than filing suit in a state which does not allow private bonding companies.

Inmate Makes a Call

As stated earlier, after a family or friend signs for a bond for the arrested person (the defendant) must visit the office of the bondsman to complete the paperwork. This paperwork states that the bond company will ensure that if the inmate is released, the inmate will attend any court hearing pertaining to the case, including roll calls and trials. This puts the bond company in jeopardy of having to pay the bond if the defendant does not appear as directed.

The fee for the bond is usually ten (10) percent of the amount of the bond. If the bond is $20,000, the person who signs on the bond will pay $2,000 to the bondsman. Many people who bond out persons do not have the entire bond fee, and the bond company will loan or finance the fee. A down payment will usually be required.

Most times a family member signs the bond, but there are times when family members do not have the money, and a friend, or current "romantic interest" will sign the bond.

I have seen the most ridiculous persons used as the signer of a bond. Remember, these people will supposedly be responsible for making sure the defendant appears in court at the appointed time. The most ridiculous signers are girlfriends of defendants.

These regular criminal customers change girlfriends more often than you change your socks. This might help when the defendant casts the girlfriend aside, but the likelihood of criminal domestic violence will keep these women from talking. This is where some "social engineering" on the part of the bondsman comes into play. Getting a signer to talk is an art.

The Signer of the Bond

The signer is responsible for paying the bond if the defendant does not show up, and the defendant becomes a fugitive. The signer will legally be responsible for the entire amount of the bond. This is a psychological ploy, and sometimes the pressure makes the signer reveal information of the whereabouts of a fleeing defendant. Most of the time, if the signer has strong allegiance with the "defendant, turned fugitive" and the liability of being the signer does not put the signer in jeopardy of losing anything, the signer will never give up the location of the fugitive, even if the fugitive is in the attic or in a closet (yes, I have seen both).

Let me explain the mind of the person signing the bond.

Most defendants do not have much money, nor do they own real estate. If the defendant does own real estate, or the signer owns real estate, the real estate will not be worth much. There will be a huge mortgage on the house, and no equity. If the bondsman sues the signer, there will not be enough equity to pay the bond, and the bondsman will not be willing to foreclose on the property, paying off the mortgage (or mortgages) just to take the property.

During the 18 months in which I was associated with the bond company, we never foreclosed upon any real estate to pay a bond because we captured all the fleeing fugitives in our system. I was very good at finding missing persons, which was a skill I had honed beginning in 1975.

The signer knows that the bond company will not come after them, so threatening to take the house of the signer is a waste of time. As a bondsman, you need to find better leverage than a civil complaint to collect the bond if the signer does not reveal the location of the fugitive.

There are ways to attach a lien to other property (as collateral) but it is too much trouble to enforce. It is easier and more cost effective to put the "boots on the ground" and pull out all the stops and find the fugitive.

Fear and intimidation were used to get information. We were nice to some people and threatened to tell authorities of criminal activity to squeeze info from others. We had informants on the ground, in the neighborhoods, and we protected those informants.

It is not unusual for a bond company to have been used to bond out a person multiple times, and on separate occasions. The defendant could have been arrested multiple times in a short span and have two or three bonds on him concurrently.

Bondsman Delivers Paperwork

After the bond fee has been paid to the bondsman, the bondsman will take paperwork copies to the clerk of court (get the papers clocked in), and a copy of the bond will be delivered (usually hand delivered so the defendant can be released quickly). The bondsman then takes another copy to the jail.

The jailers will send the paperwork to the appropriate place within the jail, and the defendant will be released. Usually the defendant will find out the release time from the jailer, so the defendant can call someone to be picked up from the jail.

After being released, the defendant will have to go to the bail bond company and sign some papers within a brief period, which is usually a day or so. These papers basically give rights to the bondsman to deny the defendant of all his civil rights to apprehend him if the defendant becomes a fugitive. This means the bondsman can break down a door to get the defendant-turned-fugitive and enter a residence without a warrant.

Denying him his civil rights means the bondsman can, and do, enter homes without knocking, busting down doors if necessary. This crazy "TV" stuff does not happen very often, but when you arrive (meaning to "roll up) to a crack house in the middle of the woods at 4:00am, the bondsman does not knock on the door. My man Tommy Martin slapped a man so hard that the man went flying across a carport as we went after a fugitive who was in the house with about 6 others. The fugitive was a female. She hid behind the door Tommy entered, and when he got in, he yelled, "The bitch got out."

Well, she ran the wrong way, and went into the back yard in pitch black darkness and ran right into the arms of another bondsman who was standing a few feet from me.

The defendant knows that when a bondsman is after him, it is about money and ego for the owner of the bond company. For the regular bondsman, employed by the owner of the company, he wants to keep his job, and he will be crazy enough and focused enough to whatever is necessary to recover the fugitive. No one wants to be fooled, and the game is likened to a predator and his prey.

Most bondsmen have a mandatory check-in for the defendants, like once a week, so the bondsmen will have up to date information on the defendant. If the defendant does not show up for his regular check-in, then it is time to make some calls to make sure the defendant had not left the area. Current information is vital to the bondsman. Establishing a pattern is the best way to predict the future activity of a person. Information is key, and the bondsman needs a lot of information.

Roll Call- Bondsman Attendance is Necessary

The defendant will be given notice from the prosecutor that the "First Appearance" in court will be a certain date after the arrest. This is the Roll Call. The first Roll Call for the defendant is usually within a month or two from being arrested. This is not a special hearing for this defendant; all criminal defendants from that jurisdiction must appear on that date. They sit and wait for their names to be called. This is also called a "cattle call" because it looks like a cattle stockyard with people shoulder to shoulder, trying to find a place to sit.

The defendant will wait in the crowded courtroom for his/her name to be called. When the name of the defendant is called, the defendant will walk down front. The defendant might have a lawyer present. The lawyer will do most of the talking. If the defendant has no lawyer, and tells the court he cannot afford a lawyer, the court will appoint a Public Defender either at that time or direct the defendant to the office of the Public Defender.

If the defendant does not appear at any roll call (either the first, second, or third), the defendant will have a big problem.

Bail Bondsmen will be found in the courtroom waiting to see if their clients (the defendants) show up. The prosecutor and the judge have a list of all defendants from which they call names. If the bondsman has a copy of the list, the bondsman will know when his client will be called.

If the defendant does not show up for Roll Call, the bondsman had better start looking for the defendant. If the bondsman does not find the defendant, it could cost the bondsman a lot of money, and the bondsman could be ordered to pay the entire bond. All hell will be breaking loose soon.

Failure to Appear

The prosecutor yells out the name of a defendant during Roll Call. No one comes down front. The prosecutor tells the judge that the defendant is not in the courtroom. After it has been determined that the defendant failed to appear at Roll Call, the prosecutor tells the judge that the office of the prosecutor requests a bench warrant.

The judge bangs the gavel, and, in effect, the judge issues a bench warrant. The bench warrant will be drafted in the office of the prosecutor, taken to the judge to be signed by the judge, and filed with the clerk of court. The bail bondsman will need to get a copy of that bench warrant before he goes to arrest the defendant. Sometimes the bail bondsman will arrest the defendant without the proper paperwork, but it is easier to have the paperwork at hand. It could take a day or two for the prosecutor to get the bench warrant drafted, presented to the judge, get it signed, and filed with the Clerk of Court.

If the defendant is not located and placed back into jail by law enforcement or the bondsman, the prosecutor can make a motion to the court to have the bondsman pay the entire bond to the court, and some of that money will be sent to the prosecutor's office.

There are occasions that law enforcement will arrest the defendant on other charges, or know the defendant has an outstanding bench warrant and happen to see the defendant.

Constant Monitoring of Defendant

If the defendant has not been brought to trial, entered a plea, or had charges dropped, the bond company will have to continue to know the whereabouts of the defendant. If the defendant did not appear in court, and the judge issues a warrant for Failure to Appear, the bondsman is given a certain amount of time to arrest the defendant before the prosecutor will ask for the entire bond be paid to the court. This time will vary from state to state. I believe in South Carolina the time is a few months. The prosecutor has the discretion to call the bond due at any time after the expiration of the original time after the warrant was issued. I have seen outstanding warrants for Failure to Appear exceed three (3) years after the defendant failed to appear at a roll call. It is all up to the prosecutor to call in the bond, and the decision- making process could be affected by friendship with the bondsman, friendship with family members of the prosecutor, deals being made for extended time, or personal grudges against the bondsman. There is never a regimented formula for calling the bond due for a fleeing defendant's bond. Calling the bond due and calling the criminal case to trial is all at the discretion of the prosecutor. This means deals are done between the prosecutor and the bail bondsman; all in the family.

Prosecutor Calling Bond Due

The prosecutor has varied reasons for allowing a defendant to remain a fugitive and not make a motion to the Court that the full amount of the bond be paid to the Court by the bonding company.

A reason for calling a bond due quickly might be the large amount of the bond, which means the fugitive was charged with a terrible crime.

In South Carolina, if the bond company pays the bond (or part of the bond), the money paid to the court by the bonding company because of a defendant becoming a fugitive is divided many ways. From what I remember (this was over 10 years ago) the percentage of the full amount of the repayment of the bond which went to the prosecutor's office was twenty-five (25) percent. If the bond company had a $50,000 bond on a fugitive, and the prosecutor wanted the bond called due because the defendant's status was that of a fugitive, and let's say the judge reduced the bond liability to

$40,000, the prosecutor's office stood to gain $10,000. The rest of the money went to the court and other places. This is a great source of revenue for the prosecutor, as well as other branches of local government.

A Valentine Present: Flowers, and Jail

One day in 2006, I noticed a bond on a black female fugitive which had been outstanding for 3 years. The prosecutor had not called the bond due. It was a roll of the dice to think the prosecutor was going to continue to ignore this, so I decided to focus on this fugitive. Her crime was forging checks.

An aunt of the defendant/fugitive was the person who signed on the bond. Of course, the amount of the bond was more than the aunt could afford to pay, but a bondsman always would say to the person who signed the bond," You know you signed the bond, and I can come after you for the full amount of the bond, take your house..." The aunt lived south of Charleston, SC, about 130 miles from the office. The aunt kept telling me that she had not seen the fugitive, but that she had seen the mother and other family members. The aunt told me that the fugitive would call her from time to time but supposedly gave no information as to her whereabouts, only that she was probably within a 60-mile radius.

The defendant was not in NCIC (National Crime Information Center database (to be explained later) and there was no indication that the female fugitive/defendant had been arrested or was serving another sentence. Since the bench warrant was not in NCIC, I decided to drive to the area south of Charleston and see the relatives.

They all said they had not seen the fugitive, and I knew they were lying, but I just wanted a snippet of something I had not heard from them in earlier conversations. During two or three trips to see the relatives, I did not learn much. I just needed to show up and put my face to their face. If I could keep the conversation going, I knew I would get a bit of information at some point.

On February 15, 2005 (you will understand why I know the exact date very soon) I called the aunt again. The calls to her were regular, she was never rude, and I was pleasant with her. We both knew she was lying to me, but I was still looking for something new. On this day, the aunt told me that she heard from a relative (another lie) that the fugitive had an argument with a boyfriend (news to me that she had a boyfriend) because the boyfriend came home to find Valentine flowers which had been given to the fugitive; the flowers came from a different man. The boyfriend got angry, loud, and shot a firearm in the house, at the fugitive. Supposedly the aunt did not know where the shooting took place, but she said it might (?) be around Charleston. The aunt was not sure if the police were called, but she thought the fugitive called the police.

If the fugitive did call the police, I knew I would find the fugitive.

I now had a house, a boyfriend, a live-in boyfriend, a shooting, the shooting was probably local, the police might have been called, and the boyfriend had a job. This was additional information.

A call was made to the City of Charleston Police. There was no record of a shooting on Valentine's Day. A call was made to the City of North Charleston, asking if a shooting had been reported. They said yes. Bingo.

I asked for the address and the name of the complainant on the incident report. The name of the person calling in the report was the same as the fugitive. I asked the record office to fax (yes, we used fax machines then) me a copy of the incident report.

The name was that of the fugitive, and the date of birth matched. Now I had an address. Maps were made, vehicles were fueled. Another bondsman (Tommy Martin, 5'6" 290 pounds, terrible attitude but loved me) went with me.

Tommy and I drove to North Charleston and found the house at approximately 3:30 pm. We did not see a car. We decided to go to Kentucky Fried Chicken and have a nice meal and discuss the plan. We never knew what could happen when we picked up a fugitive. We called our office to advise that we were "going in" soon.

We went back to the residence at approximately 4:00pm and found a truck in the driveway. I pulled along the left side of the truck. A man was sitting in the truck, and a female was standing outside the truck driver door. The female was wearing a nightgown. We emerged from our vehicle and approached the vehicle. Tommy said the name of the defendant as I walked behind the defendant. The man in the truck said, "Who the (bleep) are you?"

Tommy stood so the driver could not open his door, and said, "You gotta go, now."

It was hard to keep from laughing, but unless the man had a gun, we knew he did not want to fight Tommy. The man in the truck drove away.

The female fugitive was very surprised. She was arrested in front of a man, in her driveway, while she was wearing a nightgown, at 4:00pm. We allowed her to go into her apartment, put on some clothes, and we took her to jail.

Sometime Tommy's confidence was so brazen that it was hard for me to ever keep a straight face when we were picking up fugitives. His nickname was "Tommy Gun" and Tommy told me that he could not tell me how he got the name.

RTSC for Bondsman

When the prosecutor decides to call a bail bond due because the defendant has been a fugitive for a while, the prosecutor will file a motion with the Clerk of Court. This motion, filed with the Court, will be put before a judge to be signed. The motion is called a "Rule to Show Cause."

In any legal proceeding, a Rule to Show cause is a document which is served upon a person by another person. The person receiving the Rule to Show cause must go to court and "show cause" or explain to the court why they should not be punished for violating an agreement or a court order.

I am going to make up a simple example of why the motion is called a Rule to Show Cause:

A man owns an aggressive dog which is loose in the neighborhood. The dog owner gets a citation for the dog being loose and is told that if the dog gets loose again, the dog owner will go to jail for 30 days. A week after the court order, the dog is loose again.

The neighbors then will contact their lawyer and draft a Rule to Show Cause to file in the Clerk of Court office and serve upon the dog owner. The Rule means this: the dog owner must show cause why he should not serve the thirty days in jail. Showing "cause" means that the owner can give a reason, or excuse, that the dog was out. The dog owner will say, "The dog was out 'because'... and give the reason, which is the "cause" of the dog being out.

The word "Rule" is used as a "demand" as if from a person of authority. Sometimes the word "rule" changes from a noun (a rule) to a verb (wanting to rule a person into court). If I am "ruling you into court" that means I have served you with a Rule to Show Cause, and you must go to court to defend yourself against violating a court order, and you must give a reason why you should not have to pay the penalty.

It sounds weird to those who are not familiar with it, but if you are ever given a court order, you better know about a Rule to Show Cause, which is sometimes called simply a "Rule".

If a man had been given a restraining order to stay away from his wife, and he continued to come back, the wife can show evidence to the police of the violation of the restraining order, and the prosecutor will have the man served with a Rule to Show Cause, to show why he should not be held in contempt of court and suffer the consequences.

The bail bonding company has a duty to deliver the defendant to the court at all the appointed times, but the bondsman is not going to sleep with each defendant to make sure they go to court.

The bondsman usually has a computer system which tells him the roll call or court date of each defendant client. The bondsman gets this information from the defendant, usually in a letter to the defendant. Days or weeks before the court date, the bondsman should be on the phone calling the defendant reminding him of the court date and making sure the defendant will be attending court. If the defendant does not appear, the bail bond company has violated their agreement with the court.

This is when the bondsman starts looking for the defendant, who is now a fugitive.

My experience was that the prosecutor can serve a Rule to Show Cause on the bonding company for upwards of 12 fugitives at once. The court date was usually 10 days to 2 weeks from the service of the Rule, which meant the bonding company had that given time to arrest the named fugitives or must stand before a judge and start giving reasons for why the defendant remained fugitive.

The prosecutor will bring the bail bond company to the court. The prosecutor will ask that the entire amount of the bond, be paid by the bail bond company.

The bondsman will appear in court before the judge. The prosecutor will make his case that the defendant is a fugitive, and that the bail bond company promised to deliver the defendant to court.

The bondsman will tell the court of all things which were done to locate the defendant, including work with law enforcement. Sometimes the prosecutor would not allow the bench warrant to be put into NCIC (which will be discussed in a later chapter) which would have assisted law enforcement in foreign jurisdictions.

NCIC warrants enable foreign law enforcement to arrest the fugitive if the fugitive was stopped by law enforcement. If the warrant is not in NCIC, only local law enforcement knows of the bench warrant.

Sometimes the arresting agency will be helpful to a bondsman. The most cooperative agency was the US Marshall's Office if the fugitive was arrested on a federal warrant. The FBI is never going to help unless the bondsman has a close and private relationship with an agent.

The bondsman will tell the judge the status of the defendant, all law enforcement agencies which are involved in the search, and other issues which affected the fact that the defendant was on the loose. The bondsman will be begging for a reduction of the full bond amount to be paid. Usually the judge cuts the bail bond company a break and makes them pay a reduced amount, or the judge can give the bondsman extra time to find the defendant, arrest him, or have him put into jail.

The prosecutor controls whether a defendant will be brought back from another state or country (which is called being extradited). Sometimes this is a personal decision on the part of the prosecutor to make the bondsman spend his resources to go to another jurisdiction and arrest the fugitive defendant rather than allow the bondsman to enlist the assistance of local law enforcement in the area where the defendant is thought to be hiding.

Fugitive Fled to Another Jurisdiction

If the bondsman finds the fugitive in a foreign jurisdiction, he will travel to the foreign jurisdiction to apprehend the fugitive. It is not a good idea to let too many people in the foreign jurisdiction know you are coming, including law enforcement. The foreign law enforcement office can be contacted immediately upon your arrival, as a courtesy, and the bondsman should make a call to let the locals know where you are in case all hell breaks loose. If the foreign law enforcement agency is relatively close, and they are trusted, the bondsman might enlist a foreign office with assisting with orientation of the area, or associates of the fugitive. The foreign law enforcement agency wants the fugitive out of their area and is usually great in assisting.

F A bail bond company does not have much of an employee interview process. Many of the bondsmen have been involved in crime (maybe not caught) but not enough to keep them from getting licensed. Bail bond companies always have sources and informants with their hands out waiting to be paid for information. You have to be a bit crazy to be a bondsman, so a bit of "crazy" is tolerated. When it is crunch time, it is the crazy guy who will be up front.

There are always former inmates calling and hanging around the bail bond company, wanting money for information. I have seen a stepmother give up her step-son on a promise of having new tires put on her car. You think I am lying? I was there, and she pointed out the room where the fugitive was hiding. We found him in a closet, after he had escaped us twice. The bottom line is the bond company must capture the fugitives before the bond is called due by the prosecutor.

LAW ENFORCEMENT

The Mission

When a police officer is engaged in the performance of his official duties, he is entrusted with civic responsibilities of the highest order. His mission is to protect the life, the liberty, and the property of the citizenry. If he violates the Federal Constitution while he is performing that mission, I believe that federal law provides the citizen with a remedy against his employer as well as a remedy against him as an individual. This conclusion is supported by the text of 42 U.S.C. 1983, by its legislative history, and by the holdings and reasoning in several of our major cases construing the statute. The Court's contrary conclusion rests on nothing more than a recent judicial fiat that no litigant had asked the Court to decree. [100]

This quote came from Justice John Paul Stevens in dissent of the case described below:

The story of Oklahoma City v. Tuttle begins with the October 4, 1980 shooting death of William Adam Tuttle. [1]

Certain facts about the shooting were not disputed. On October 4, 1980, Officer Julian Rotramel responded to a report of an armed robbery in progress at the We'll Do Club, a tavern in Oklahoma City. He entered the building and saw that no armed robbery was taking place and was told by the bartender that there had been no such robbery. However, Tuttle approached Rotramel who recognized that he fit the "robber's" description, and Rotramel ordered him to remain in the bar. When Tuttle subsequently disobeyed that order and left the building, Officer Rotramel fatally shot him.

Beyond these basic facts, the parties sharply disagreed about what happened and the reasons for the shooting. Officer Rotramel claimed that he shot Tuttle because of a reasonable, albeit erroneous, belief that Tuttle was reaching for a gun and was about to shoot him. The plaintiff, on the other hand, portrayed the shooting as an unjustified shooting by an ill-trained officer.

Tuttle's widow sued both Officer Rotramel and Oklahoma City and the jury handed down an oddly split verdict. It found for Officer Rotramel (apparently on the basis that he was therefore to qualified immunity), but found against the City and awarded Ms. Tuttle $1,500,000 damages (apparently on the basis that the City's training of police officers was grossly negligent). The Court of Appeals affirmed both aspects of the verdict.

In the Supreme Court, the city successfully challenged the trial court's instructions on inadequate training, and the case was sent back to the trial court for a new trial with proper instructions. The city prevailed on retrial, and Ms. Tuttle was awarded nothing.

Officer Rotramel was cleared of wrongdoing by the Oklahoma City Police Department Firearms Review Board, but he left the force the next year. He is now an accountant. [101]

Justice Stevens dissented in the case. The law enforcement agency was found not to be liable, using the excuse of inadequate training. Inadequate training was used as an excuse in another other case before the US Supreme Court when the prosecutor's office of New Orleans was sued.

It is shocking that both prosecutors and law enforcement use the same excuse for not being liable for misconduct. It is also shocking, in my humble and less educated opinion, that Title 42 Section 1983 is rarely enforced and causes no anxiety on the part of law enforcement or prosecutors.

Remember that one of the fallacies of the criminal justice system, as stated by Judge Alex Kozinski, is: *"Police are objective in their investigations."* [102]

Qualified Immunity

Very rarely does a law enforcement officer witness a crime in progress. I am not referring to seeing a kid selling a joint of marijuana, or someone passing a packet of drugs into a car, or even a shootout at a laundromat. Most crimes are reported after the fact or not during the commission of the crime. Maybe an officer has a suspicion, or just maybe a vendetta will generate interest in beginning an investigation. This is fertile ground for corruption. For those in law enforcement who feel squeamish about seeing or knowing about corruption among fellow officers, considering the fact that that the corrupt officer has a family at home to support and a job which they love, this can be a very uncomfortable situation.

The honest cop, if he is intuitive at all (he should be if he wants to be a cop), will be able to tell the good guys from the bad guys most of the time, especially those with whom he works. There are those who fool fellow cops, as FBI agent Connolly, who was associated with mobster Whitey Bulger in Boston. If a cop has a feeling that one of his brother cops is dirty, he must decide if he will tell someone, but that person might be dirty, too. The dirty cops make the job of being a cop more difficult for those who are good cops. I have respect for the good ones, but here we will focus on the job the cop is supposed to do, and some of the bad ones.

I know both the good and the bad.

The good cops do a fantastic and heroic job. Even the bad cops perform heroic acts. They have my respect and admiration for saving lives and protecting people on the street, not for screwing them over.

Below are some of the issues which the new officer will face.

Bright-Eyed at the Beginning

The men and women who graduate from a law enforcement academy are bright eyed, have the visions of our flag, dream of saving innocent citizens from criminals, and locking the criminals away. Some have had military service and have had experience in confrontation. Some of this experience, sad to say, will be with a group in which corruption has been evident. The psychological tests might pick up "crazy" but not pick up "dirty."

Many Become Corrupt

I employed at least 5 former law enforcement officers as private investigators. I asked one what percentage of law enforcement is corrupt; he told me at least 60 percent. If the new officer is not aware of the culture, the new officer will be swallowed up by it.

It is obvious that people take a job because they "want that job."

People who want to be in law enforcement don't give themselves a wide range of other options. Law enforcement is what they want. Young people go to work at a fast food restaurant with the anticipation of this being a temporary job. That is not the case with law enforcement.

Law Enforcement Impacts Many

Once they get there, the culture is very hands on. There are meetings, training, reviews, and in proximity to their immediate superior. Pleasing their boss serves different purposes: it strokes the ego of the boss and allows the young cop to keep his job. These two reasons for pleasing a boss might seem universal, but pleasing the boss in a law enforcement setting has a difference; This job affects the lives of:

The cop
The cop's family
The victim
The victim's family
The defendant and his family

There is more pressure on law enforcement than any other member of the criminal justice family. If the cops don't get it right, no one gets arrested, no crime is solved, the crime will happen again.

This pressure can and does erode at the conscience of many in law enforcement. The pressure can come from the supervisor or self-imposed pressure to solve the case. This pressure, and the erosion of conscience, is passed down from rank to rank, from a supervisor to his people. If the supervisor is dirty, the supervisor will allow and encourage the same behavior from those who serve under him.

The pressure to attain the rank of the supervisor is great, and you do not want to go to a meeting and announce to everyone that your supervisor is dirty. If you do that, you will be in a different line of work very soon.

Along with eroding the conscience of the law enforcement officer, pressure will also cause the officer to make mistakes, or report something inaccurate either by mistake or in an attempt to fool the defense.

I used knowledge of that pressure to my advantage as I would pick apart a law enforcement report to find mistakes which helped my client. As a PI doing criminal defense work, the first thing I did was to read as much as I could from law enforcement reports to find mistakes, omissions, leading statements, laziness, and false charges. I had the luxury of propping my feet on my desk, reading a police report in perfectly quiet surroundings, maybe some coffee on my desk, as I relaxed to read.

Law enforcement officers write reports under a lot of pressure. Mistakes are made. The cops were not relaxed when they wrote the report. Their boss was up their ass.

It is with certainty that those in law enforcement will have to make a choice many times in their career whether to be dirty or be clean. Once they start being dirty, and they get over the guilt, their conscience becomes eroded and they will feel no guilt.

The following three short stories are examples of laziness and corruption.

Shotgun Suicide

In the spring of 1986, a black lady came into my office. She told me that the sheriff's department told her that her brother had committed suicide over the previous Thanksgiving holiday. Supposedly, they found her brother dead in his mobile home. Her concern was that her brother had recently spoken to her from the grave and told her that he did not kill himself. She needed to be consoled, so I told her I would look into it.

While I did not come to any conclusion that there was foul play, I did find out that the shotgun found near the body had been later propped up next to a filing cabinet (I saw it) in the sheriff's office, and was never examined. When I went to talk to the coroner, he showed me the photographs of the scene; the photographs were in an open letter-sized envelope, and on the front seat of his pick-up truck. He showed me the photos while we sat in his truck, as he ate his lunch. Yes, he ate his lunch while we looked at the photos of a man having shot his brains out, with blood and brains spattered all over a wall.

The coroner told me that no autopsy had been performed. Months later, I learned that the coroner told someone that no one would die in that county again without having had an autopsy. Sounds like a good idea, huh?

Was it not odd that the shotgun had not been examined for 6 months, having been stuck in a corner, and the photographs of the dead man had been on the front seat of the coroner's pick-up truck (he had been showing the ghastly photos to anyone interested)? The sheriff of that county, who I dealt with personally on this case, would, years later be found picking up trash along a highway as punishment for using free jail labor to do work at his home. The first name of the sheriff was Bubba. Really, his name was Bubba.

A Mother Thought She Killed Her Daughter

A lady was traveling on a major highway as she approached an intersection. The highway was a normal four lane highway, with separate inside left turn lanes for each direction. Each turn lane had a turn signal/arrow. The turn signal for the turn lanes on the major highway was controlled by a "stop bar" which was located in median of the highway, marked with a wide white line which was perpendicular to the flow of traffic.

The side streets intersecting the major highway had 2 lanes and had no median.

A stop bar is approximately six feet long and two feet wide and is placed in the median of the left turn lane at five or six car lengths from the intersection. Cars drive across the stop bar, in the turn lane, as they approach the turn signal. When the signal turns green, a computer will detect cars crossing the stop bar. If there are six or seven cars (the axles are counted as they cross the stop bar) which cross the stop bar, the turn signal will remain green for a longer period, probably 15-20 seconds. (This case was over 15 years ago, so my timing might be off a little.) The computer will allow only a certain number of cars to pass before the signal turns yellow. If no cars are detected crossing the stop bar, the computer will know that traffic is not backing up, and the turn signal will be on for a shorter amount of time.

The yellow turn light will be on for about 5 seconds. After the yellow light goes out, all the lights across the intersection will be red. All lights at the intersection will be red for 4 seconds to allow all vehicles to "clear the intersection" before any green light is illuminated. These lights and programmed times are important to the case.

The lady driver had a passenger. The passenger was a daughter who was about 8 years old, who was seated in the front passenger seat.

As the lady approached the intersection, her intention was to turn left. There were probably 5 cars ahead of her. She stopped in the median turn lane behind the other cars as the turn light was red. As the turn signal became green, the cars in the turn lane began turning left.

When the lady turned left, entering the intersection, she was hit broadside by a logging truck on the passenger side of the car. Her daughter was killed. The lady was charged with ignoring the red signal, implying that the turn signal on the traffic light was red, and that she should have stopped. The highway patrolman stated that the mother was responsible for the death of her daughter.

The lady swore that her turn light was not red.

When I got the case, I learned about the stop bar, the computer, the lights, and the timing from the department of transportation. We videoed the sequence of the changing lights at the intersection. We timed the lights. We talked to the engineers at the department of transportation. This was not enough.

I had to talk to witnesses. The sound of the crash was so loud that the drivers ahead of the lady had stopped and came back to the scene. The fact that some drivers returned to the scene helped solve the case.

Two drivers who turned left immediately ahead of the lady returned to the scene. Both stated that their turn light was yellow. That is believable because if the yellow light was on for 5 seconds, at least 2 cars could have passed under a yellow light.

This brought me to the red light, and the revelation to me which solved the case and overturned the charge against the lady. If the driver ahead of the lady had a yellow light, and if mother-driver did in fact have a red light, then immediately after the yellow light was out, all lights at the intersection were red for 4 seconds, allowing all traffic to clear the intersection. This amount of time was enough to allow the lady to clear the intersection. All lights were red by design.

Our investigation proved the logging truck did not have–enough time to travel through the intersection and gain enough speed to hit the car and kill the young girl. The logging truck would not have been able to accelerate fast enough to cause the damage which killed the young girl.

The only way the logging truck could have inflicted that much damage was if the driving lane in front of the log truck was clear, and the log truck was approaching the intersection, timing the light in order not to have to stop. The logging truck driver could have seen that the light for cross traffic was turning yellow to red, and he did not consider that all lights would be red for 4 seconds in order to clear the intersection.

My report was submitted. The traffic violation was reversed, and the lady was no longer made to feel that she caused the death of her daughter.

The logging truck driver was then charged with the violation, and the death of the young girl.

This was one of the most satisfying cases I handled. It seemed to be an ordinary traffic accident involving a fatality.

Cops Drinking en route to the Bowling Alley

At about 6:00pm on a winter night, the sky was dark, and a heavy drizzle was falling. Cars were using their headlights and windshield wipers. A group of law enforcement officers from a rural area were traveling south on a four-lane highway on their way to a bowling alley. The group, in two cars, one behind the other, were traveling south on the inside passing lane. There were no cars to their right, which made a person wonder why both cars would be in the passing lane unless they were in a hurry. Both cars were personal cars, not police cars.

The driver of the first car was the ex-wife of a highway patrol officer and was a clerk in the sheriff's office. Another occupant was the chief deputy of that sheriff department. A backseat passenger was a nineteen-year-old secretary of the department. Alcohol was being drunk in the car, which was against the law as a passenger and the nineteen-year-old female.

Suddenly, the front car hit something.; the object struck was a person, and the victim came crashing into the car, through the windshield, and landed next to the driver, on the console.

One witness stated that a leg of the victim was severed and flew into the air. The driver screamed. I would have screamed, too.

It was determined that the victim was under the influence of drugs, and after that was determined, law enforcement washed their hands of the matter.

I found out from witnesses that after the impact, the second car of law enforcement officers stopped behind the vehicle which struck the pedestrian. Officers from both vehicles emerged from their respective vehicle and began carrying beer and wine cooler bottles from the first car and putting the alcohol in the second car while the dying man was lying in the first car. This was witnessed by firefighters who arrived immediately after the impact. The fire station was a few hundred yards from the scene of the accident, and they heard the tires squealing and could see an accident had occurred.

The statements from the firefighters were damaging to the law enforcement officers, but more needed to be done. I found the wrecked car in a junk yard. I was able to get into the junk yard and inspect the car. Guess what I found on the floor in the wrecked car? I found a bottle cap from a wine cooler bottle, just as described by the fire fighter.

The problem not only was that the officers were drinking, but the under aged employee in the back seat had also been drinking. The cover up was also an issue, as well as the lies about the alcohol.

It took almost a year before any of the officers were held accountable. The officers were reprimanded by the sheriff, which meant nothing.

Technology has changed traffic accident investigations and criminal investigations. This has helped solve crime as well as free wrongly incarcerated defendants. DNA testing had other new scientific procedures have helped solve crimes.

Expert Witnesses

Objective information is what you want. The word "opinion" implies being subjective. In a courtroom setting, you will always find each side presenting an expert who will take objective information and interpret it to suit their agenda. The prosecution and the defense will present their biased witnesses. After a person obtains a certain amount of education and experience in a certain discipline (law enforcement, forensics, psychiatric, etc.) they can create a resume which they shop around to prosecution and defense attorneys. These "experts" will be contacted by either side of the case and determine what testimony they would give, or what testimony they "will" give. Experts can and are groomed to give testimony to help who pays them.

Remember the case I mentioned about the lady who was the boot construction expert, and testified what she was told to say? It happens. It is all about fooling a jury.

Yes, the experts get paid. Of course, they usually have a business of their own, and it is difficult to schedule an exact time the expert will be testifying, which means the expert loses money from their business as they are "on hold" or waiting at the courthouse. Expert witnesses are important, but again, if two experts disagree, the "facts" seem to become subjective.

Some persons are professional courtroom experts. That is their job.

Law Enforcement Personnel Job Changes

If a law enforcement officer moves from one jurisdiction to another, holding the same rank or going to a smaller law enforcement organization, this officer was probably caught doing something really stupid at work. Most cops don't get fired; they "are allowed to resign." This is done so they can keep their pension and be hired immediately because they have been to the academy and are certified. This is a well- known secret among those in this field, within the family.

It takes a lot to get fired. If the police chief or the sheriff can keep it quiet, the officer won't have to leave. But, if a prostitute takes your service weapon, if you get drunk and fire off a few rounds into the ceiling of a restaurant, or ultimately embarrass the boss, you might get fired. If the infraction is something they can cover up, and they will cover it up, it will not be in your record, and the officer will be allowed to resign.

Cover ups are the name of the game in law enforcement, which is why a plea agreement is so important. My book, Don't Get Arrested in South Carolina, detailed an extensive cover up by 3 police agencies, simultaneously, of the involvement of a former law enforcement officer in a death. This case also resulted in a different type of cover up when a law enforcement agency, which investigated a death, refused to honor a Freedom of Information Request for the records of the case. We got the charges dropped after a two-and-a-half-year fight. I made few friends on that case.

In another case, the accidental death of a man who swallowed a small bag of cocaine (it was learned he did this at a traffic stop/license check on his way home after making the "buy,") resulted in the halting of the investigation when law enforcement began to determine the origin of the cocaine. Records were subpoenaed from the sheriff's department, but the records were never given up. I found out that the cocaine was delivered by a female "coke whore" who was well known by law enforcement and had been having sex with some of the officers. This same female had 3-4 relationships with men prior to the man who swallowed the coke, and all those prior relationships resulted in prison or death (drug related, or suspicious) for the men. This female was also responsible for having law enforcement officers plant cocaine in the car of a current boyfriend. The father of this person was known to me and was a former law enforcement officer. The boyfriend never used the drug, but it was planted in his car at a restaurant.

I talked to the victim, and he told me who he thought planted the drugs. I told him I probably knew the dirty cop and gave the victim the initials. The reply from the victim was, "How did you know?" Having been in the investigative business for decades, I knew some dirty cops, and dirty cop bosses.

The arrest was strictly for vengeance. I knew the name of the officer who planted the cocaine. Believe me; I am not making this up.

Law enforcement officers are not lawyers. The only law enforcement officer I knew who went to law school was one of my employees. He did not want to be a lawyer; he wanted to be a cop, so he went to law school and became a cop. I was at his wedding.

I can assure you, wherever he is, he is still a good cop. Some members of law enforcement try to interpret the law, and act as a buffer between a victim and the prosecutor. They do it because they "can."

The Brush-Off

There are times when the public feel they were the victim of a crime, whether it was financial, physical, or other. The victim will go to the police and tell the story, and the police might tell them "this is not a crime. You need to go hire a lawyer," or " this is civil, not criminal." This brush off (which I have heard many times from victims, and directly from law enforcement) is a result of the law enforcement not knowing the criminal statute (which is not their job), not understanding the issues, or just plain laziness.

I never expected law enforcement to have memorized the state or federal statutes. They must write a report showing which law has been broken or tell the prosecutor the events of an arrest for the prosecutor to write up a warrant. There are some ordinary statutes which relate to crimes that occur frequently, and law enforcement officers might know that statute. But, if the victim feels the perpetrator violated a crime of which the law enforcement is not very familiar, or needs to interpret the code of laws, again, law enforcement will brush off the victim and tell them to get a lawyer because "this is civil and not criminal."

I have many cases to law enforcement on behalf of victims, even presenting a printed copy of the law. The victim had better have all documentation and basically solve the crime themselves before they present the case. This is true for state and federal law enforcement.

Bobbi Brazzell, Identity Theft, and the Lazy Sheriff's Investigator

Around 2002, a female friend, named Bobbi Brazzell, called me and told me she and a female friend went to a bar; and they put their pocketbooks into the trunk of the car. Somehow a thief broke into the trunk of the car and stole their pocketbooks.

A few weeks later, Bobbi began getting letters from banks, stating that she had bounced checks. These were bank accounts which she did not own. Bobbi reported this to the sheriff department after being made to fill out affidavits of forgery at the banks for each bounced check.

Bobbi called me because she kept getting daily letters from the banks and the sheriff department was doing nothing. The banks were asking for monies to be repaid, as well as bank fees. As the letters mounted, she realized that the bogus accounts had her correct name, Bobbi Brazzell, and her correct home address. The thief had Bobbi's home address, and she was scared to death. That is why she called me.

I researched the checks, went to the locations where the checks had been presented, pulled up store video, and finally found a person who recognized the criminal. I researched the criminal and found him living in a mobile home about 50 miles from Bobbi's apartment.

I put the case together, including checks, photos of the criminal, and photos and maps of his residence. The package was taken to the sheriff department. They did nothing. The big fat sergeant was useless, lazy, and ignorant.

One day I received a call from a grocery store located almost 80 miles from the home of the criminal. The criminal had tried to buy groceries at the store, and as the clerk was getting the check approved, the criminal got nervous, and ran out. For some reason, my name came up as a person working on the case (maybe my name came from a bank officer). I went to the store and got the identification card used by the criminal. The criminal thought no one would know who he was. I already knew his true identity.

I found out that the criminal had gone onto a website and had an identification card printed, using a photo of the criminal, and the address of Bobbi Brazzell. The ID also had Bobbi's driver license information, and other identifying information. The ID looked just like a South Carolina driver license. This is what the criminal was using to open bank accounts. The criminal had a check writing program in his mobile home, on his computer, and created checks using Bobbi's name, which the thief was using as his name, and his new identification card allowed it to happen. The funny part was that the real Bobbi Brazzell was a white female, and the criminal was a black man. The physical description on the fake identification card had the physical traits of the criminal but had Bobbi's address and name. Now you have a black man named Bobbi Brazzell. He was passing himself off as being gay.

Back to the sheriff department I went. Still, the sergeant would not listen. I then went to the FBI and irritated an FBI agent friend until he agreed to consider it since the crime involved bank fraud. Ultimately, the FBI arrested the criminal and he did big time in prison.

Therefore, I know that if you are a victim of a crime, most of the time you must sell yourself as a victim to law enforcement before anything gets done. Then you must solve the case yourself.

The Informant, aka Snitch, and the Cop

As I read the essay by Professor Natapoff, I agree with many of her observations but few of her opinions.

One issue is her assertion that using snitches creates crime. Even if (on a state level) law enforcement turns a blind eye to crimes committed by a good snitch, the law enforcement will benefit from the crimes by way of payoffs. This way the snitch has leverage over the law enforcement. It becomes a balancing act. The cop can get the informant to perform criminal acts which are too dangerous for the cop to perform, like theft or murder.

The big leverage law enforcement has over a snitch who wants to go "rogue" and tell stories about law enforcement involvement involved crime, is a gun and a rumor. The snitch knows that if he gets a bit too mouthy about "ratting out" law enforcement, it is easy to have a snitch killed. No one will make a fuss. Newspapers will not print a news item about a dead snitch.

One reason different law enforcement agencies do not share information is because they are very jealous of their snitches. I do agree with Ms. Natapoff on this point. Both the law enforcement "handler" and the snitch, together, are like a husband and wife who are running a criminal enterprise. The husband will give the wife all she wants to hide his activity.

Contrary to Ms. Natapoff, there are a good percentage of opportunistic members of law enforcement who are looking for that extra buck or the thrill of controlling an informant. These cops were born dirty and hide it well from most of their colleagues. Snitches did not create a dirty cop.

Burning an Informant

If a cop is ever found to have burned an informant, the cop will not be effective on the street. The people in the housing projects know the cops and the bail bondsman. The bail bondsman's life depends upon the informants and had better not burn one. People on the street trust the bail bondsman more than they trust law enforcement.

Drug activity and property crimes are the most useful types of data informants can give law enforcement. Assaults and murder probably are next in volume. We always needed informants to help find fugitives.

I did missing person work beginning in 1975, and was very good at it, doing it BC (before computers). I always said that solving those cases took skill and dot connecting, but there are times that the dots are your sources. You are only as good as your sources. You might have an idea where to go to get the information, but if you cannot crack the source, you have nothing. I knew how to solve a problem, and I had my sources. Even though some were as smart as me, my sources gave me an advantage.

This is the same with informants. Although law enforcement can get records faster and easier than most PI's, informants are necessary.

Flipping a Defendant or a Former Inmate

Once a criminal is flipped, and becomes an informant, law enforcement has the ultimate leverage. Outing an informant to his neighborhood will get the criminal killed. If a cop uses an informant and outs him, the cop is in danger, too. I have seen it happen.

Maybe someone is giving the cops a bunch of trouble. Cops can plant a rumor that a person is a snitch, and that person disappears.

Charlie Shivers, the Dead Informant

I was retained to defend a group of 6 black defendants on minor drug trafficking charges, and all lived in the same housing project. It looked to me like the informant lived in the project, and his name was Charlie Shivers.

I went to an apartment where a defendant thought Charlie lived. I was going to shake him up a little. The time was about 2:30pm. When I knocked on the door, I found a very young skinny black lady, wearing a thin nightgown. She was holding a snotty-nosed kid, and two more were on the floor. I told her who I was. She said Charlie lived there, and asked me to come in. There was no place I was going to sit, or touch. I told the lady that the cop at the preliminary hearing of the six defendants told the court that they had an informant (Charlie) who had no record and had never been arrested. The lady laughed and went into the kitchen, reached to take a piece of paper off the top of the refrigerator, and gave me the paper. The paper was a copy of a warrant, stating that Charlie had sold drugs to an undercover cop as the cop was sitting in his car. Charlie was kind of stupid. Charlie had been arrested in another city, fewer than 5 miles from where the defendants were arrested.

The prosecutor at the preliminary hearing either never thought to check Shivers' record or did not care about telling a lie in court.

The lady then told me that Charlie had been beating her, regularly. She would call the cops; sometimes they would come, sometimes not. If they came, they would take Charlie away and he would be gone a while, but never arrested.

I promised the young black girl I would do what I could to help her. I could see in her face that she trusted me, and she was scared.

Later, I found a witness who saw the cops arrive at the back of a bowling alley located about a mile from the housing project. The cop car stopped, and the cops let Charlie out of the back of the cop car. The cop car drove off, and Charlie walked away.

On the first day of the trial, I knew that Charlie would be at the courthouse. Preliminary motions were being filed, and a jury was being chosen. There was no need for me to be at the courthouse. This was perfect for my plan.

I went to Charlie's apartment. I found the mother of his children and got a neighbor to baby-sit the kids. I put the lady into my car and took her to the local police station. This was the same police station which officers would fake the arrest of Charlie after he beat this woman, and release Charlie at the bowling alley.

I demanded Charlie be arrested. The lady was brave enough to stand up and tell what had been happening. We got the warrant for Charlie's arrest.

I took the lady home, and then went to court. Charlie was sitting next to the prosecutor, dressed in an ill-fitting suit. No one knew what I had done, and I told no one.

The next day, I went to court. Charlie was not wearing his blue suit; Charlie was wearing an orange jumpsuit, compliments of the county jail. He had been arrested on the charges which we insisted he be charged The public defender came up to me immediately, asking what the hell I had done. I smiled. The prosecutor shot a nasty look at me. I told the defense lawyer I had evidence the cops were lying,

and promising different things to the residents of the housing project for them to implicate each other, but Charlie was the only one who took the bait. I told the lawyer that the cops then covered for Charlie beating his wife.

The judge made the jury leave the courtroom before I testified. I told the judge about the cops allowing Charlie to beat his wife as an excuse to find out about marijuana being smoked and tiny amounts traded and sold. The prosecution team was very angry at me. The judge allowed my testimony, and I presented the testimony before the jury.

In the end, the first defendant was found not guilty. Charges were dropped against all other defendants. I got a hug from the defendant, not the prosecutor.

A few weeks later, a former defendant from the housing project called me. I was told that Charlie had gotten out of jail and went back to his apartment. As Charlie was standing at the trunk of his car, a man came out of Charlie's apartment and shot Charlie, killing him. Karma is a bitch.

THE DEFENDANT

The Colorful Family Member

A defendant is a person who has been arrested. Most criminals get caught. The criminal gets lazy and might continue the same pattern of criminal behavior because "it works" and the criminal will not change the pattern. Not all defendants are criminals.

People become defendants for assorted reasons. Lack of education has been said to cause a person to turn to crime because the criminal cannot get a job, but this theory is discounted when the criminal drops out of school or does not apply himself in school. That is laziness, which carries over into the criminal life, and will result in being arrested. That is lack of focus. Peer pressure can be an issue. Most violent crime is committed by these less educated persons. These persons were probably criminals before dropping out of school.

White collar crime is committed usually by persons of higher education and higher intellect. Greed is the major factor. They want a higher station in life, giving them respect, and it takes money to do this. These persons want things which are not theirs to have and get a thrill cheating people.

White collar criminals want new friends to impress; criminals from the "hood" keep the same friends, and flash their bounty to their same friends, remaining in the same neighborhood because most of their crimes are low reward.

In most low-income areas, a person having a criminal record suffers no stigma, and no one looks down on you, or differently at you.

You did some time; you went to college (prison). Now you are educated. It's cool. Almost all your friends have a record. It is treated as a joke.

For most of these guys (mostly guys) going to jail or doing a bit of time is "the cost of doing business." This is like someone hauling drugs and having to throw some out from time to time. Sometimes you get caught, you go away a while, and you come back.

Some guys call jail their "vacation" because they get fed, they don't have to go to work, and they are with their friends. To some, it is a lifestyle. Many cannot function on the outside.

Two incidents come to mind. Once, while booking someone into a jail, a black male yelled from the booking area through the glass toward a general population area, "Wazzup my nigga?" He was home. Everyone laughed.

Another funny incident happened in the same booking area. A large wooden desk was in a corner, opposite the large entry door. A huge black male officer was processing incoming arrested persons. At least a dozen chairs were backed against a wall opposite the booking officer, and all the chairs were occupied by future inmates and the persons who arrested them. A black male had just been booked in. After being fingerprinted, the black male (new inmate) was told to grab a plastic-wrapped bologna sandwich from a pile in a blue plastic container, along with a carton of orange flavored drink, which was from a stack of small cartons next to the sandwich container. The officer spun around in his chair, preparing to wave at the control center through the glass wall, to have the big sliding door open so the new inmate could enter the population area.

As the officer was about to get the attention of the control room, the inmate picked up the bologna sandwich and asked the booking officer, "You got a microwave for this?" The place fell out laughing hysterically. The officer yelled back at the inmate, telling him there was nothing to warm up his sandwich, and that the inmate had better eat it quickly. It was pure jail language and was funny as hell. The inmate was home.

While this was a funny story, the sad part is most of the inmates are there for minor drug crimes or crimes committed to get insignificant amounts of drugs. These guys were poor. Probably 80 percent were unemployed.

Once you get arrested, you will be pressured to give up information or be the victim of a "shakedown" by the police. This means that the cops will find you on the street, knowing you are holding a small volume of drugs, and make you give up your drugs and cash in exchange for not being arrested. No one will be able to prove what happened. The cops have all the leverage.

The prison business is all about drug crimes.

Much has been written in an earlier chapter with respect to the relationship between the defendant and the bail bondsman, and I will review some of that relationship here.

After the defendant is arrested, he gets a bail hearing. A bail amount is set, and the defendant needs a bail bond company to post the bail, which is basically a promise by the bonding company to pay the bail if the defendant does not appear at scheduled court appearances. The defendant will have regularly scheduled appearances also at the bonding company, usually weekly.

If the defendant does not show up at the regularly scheduled time at the bail bonding company, the bonding company should start worrying. Calls will start being made to the residence of the defendant, and maybe a visit to the house. The sooner the bonding company gets to the defendant, the better the chances of determining why the defendant did not show up, and if he has run away. The defendant knows that running is not a promising idea.

If the defendant misses a Roll Call court appearance or a scheduled visit with a probation officer, a bench warrant will be issued. When the defendant is arrested by law enforcement or the bail bondsman, the defendant will go back to jail. The defendant will again be brought before a judge for a bond hearing, and the whole game begins again, except the defendant had another charge against him, which is Failure to Appear.

If a defendant goes back to jail as a result of a bench warrant for Failure to Appear for Roll Call, it is almost always because the bail bondsman found the defendant. If the defendant, who would be a fugitive for failing to appear, is arrested for a different crime by law enforcement, law enforcement would not know of the outstanding warrant until the fugitive was arrested.

The defendant can be in trouble with the bonding company for breaking the bonding contract. Technically, any violation of the bond is just cause to put the defendant back in jail. That was threatened to some defendants by me but it was never carried out. This violation of bond conditions could be for failing to check in, moving without telling the bonding company, or failing to pay the moneys owed to the bonding company.

If a defendant gets out of jail, does not take a plea, and appears in court for all his roll calls, the criminal case could drag for a year or more. Most courts are backed up with cases which can be good for

the defendant if the defendant was going to take a plea. The prosecutor wants the case off the desk.

Defendant might become a snitch. This involves law enforcement, prosecutor, and defense attorney. Snitches are mostly involved with law enforcement and the defendant. More about the relationship with snitches is found in the chapter involving law enforcement and the defendant.

Once arrested, the defendant had a good chance of losing his job. Many of the jobs are unskilled, some semi-skilled, and bosses will fire a defendant if he misses work, or sometimes just because he was arrested. This puts the defendant in a situation where he might commit more crime just to eat.

Becoming a defendant has major drawbacks, especially if the defendant is innocent.

THE DEFENSE ATTORNEY

Prosecutors Want Power

Have you ever wondered why attorneys who were prosecutors become private attorneys? It is the money.

Power and money are obtained for several reasons, whether you are a prosecutor or defense attorney.

Defense Attorneys Want Money

The only thing other than money (success) that a defense attorney wants is personal leverage.

Attorneys who have been prosecutors know persons in the prosecutor's office and can approach them with a plea deal. The prosecutor just wants a conviction and not to go to court. They use each other to further their careers while the defendant becomes a casualty of that relationship.

Brady Motion Procedure

The first thing the defense attorney does is draft the Brady Motion to be served upon the prosecutor. This was explained in an earlier section, but I will repeat part of this issue. After the Brady Motion is served upon the Prosecutor, the Defense Attorney should receive all evidence in the possession of the prosecutor which is favorable to the defense. Technically information in the file that is <u>material and relevant</u> in the defense of the defendant. The Defense Attorney should be smart enough to determine if there might be information in that file which he was not given.

This is when the Defense Attorney must hire, or the Defendant hire, a good PI to find out if the Prosecutor is hiding something. If something is being hidden, the Defense Attorney must file a Motion to Compel and ask the judge to order the Prosecutor to give up the hidden information. If the defense attorney is good enough and has the power to show a bit of bravado, the defense attorney can accuse the prosecutor of all kinds of misconduct and ask for the charges to be dismissed, and the prosecutor be punished with sanctions.

If the defense attorney can paint the prosecutor as a dirty rat to a fair judge, the defense attorney has a good chance of the judge will be impatient with the dirty prosecutor during a trial.

This is politics, the game, and has nothing to do with guilt or innocence. Ninety percent of the time, the prosecutor knows the defense attorney is going to say something which would offend you and me. The prosecutor and defense attorney wink and nod at one another just like fighters in professional wrestling. Their arguments do not seem real.

I have seen an unethical defense attorney file a Brady Motion on behalf of his client (the Defendant) and not receive the file after seven (7) months. This was a very high-profile case, and the unethical defense attorney was intent upon delivering the Defendant to the Prosecutor in order to gain favor with the Prosecutor. The defense attorney had been a prosecutor (never given any big cases) and wanted his claim to fame to be that he and the prosecutor were friends. The defendant became a sacrificial lamb, offered up by the defense attorney. The defense attorney had no intention of getting the evidence from the prosecutor.

He was going to squeeze out a plea from the defendant. The defense attorney told the defendant not to hire a private investigator. This defense attorney was a dirty as they come. The defendant paid the defense attorney $5,000 for nothing. The defendant fired the defense attorney, got his file, and the only thing in the file folder was the Brady Motion and newspaper clippings. The defendant did hire a private investigator, fired two more attorneys (he had 4 in all) and the prosecutor's office called the PI a few years later, agreeing to drop all charges. I was the PI.

Another defense attorney, who bragged that he never lost a case, was intent upon getting a plea from a defendant who was charged with a crime which he denied. A Brady Motion was served upon the prosecutor. The defense attorney pressured the defendant into taking a plea, telling him there was no way to win. There were three affidavits given by three witnesses, and the defendant was sure he could battle against these affidavits. The affidavits were used as probable cause to generate search warrants. The defense attorney was successful in getting the defendant to take a plea. The defendant never saw the affidavits. The defendant never had a chance to defend himself. After being in prison, the prosecutor refused to reveal the affidavits to the defendant.

It is a very touchy issue as whether a defense attorney can be aggressive with the other family members (prosecutor and law enforcement) because he will need favors from the other parties. If the defense attorney goes after the prosecutor for misconduct, he will alienate the prosecutor and not be able to get the plea agreements for the defendant, or future defendants. The defense attorney cannot be too aggressive with law enforcement.

He will need information and favors from them in the future. Bail bondsmen can refer (quietly) a specific lawyer to a defendant, but that is usually illegal.

If the defense attorney is hired by enough high paying defendants, he will not need the "favors" but can use his power to pressure the other family members to do what he wants. The defense attorney can have great power against an unprepared prosecutor. In my first murder trial, we had the prosecutor almost believing that the defendant could not have committed the crime. She seemed unsure. As soon as she seemed a bit timid, the chief prosecutor took over the case. It is all about power, favors, and money.

One client of mine was arrested for making illegal liquor. He said he paid his lawyer $20,000. Half of the money, as he was told by his defense attorney, went to the prosecutor; all cash. The defendant told me this.

If the defendant has enough money, and the case is high profile, the defense attorney can make a huge amount of money by trying the case. This is fun for the defendant because he knows he cannot win, but the defense attorney gets paid for going through the motions and gets free publicity. The defendant is entitled to a defense, but sometimes the defense is worthless. A defendant in a high-profile case just wants to get out of jail (physically) and go on a "field trip" to the courthouse. Eventually, the defendant will be found guilty, and he will go to prison and the field trips will be over.

Most defense attorneys cover up misconduct on the part of prosecutor, and never reports misconduct to the bar. The fraternity is too small, and they all are part of the same club (family).

Defense attorneys will rarely report misconduct of law enforcement. You make an enemy of law enforcement, and your life can be a living hell.

If the defendant is in jail, not bonded out, the defendant has limited phone privileges which are good for the defense attorney. No one likes an excitable chatty defendant, calling the defense attorney all the time, and if the defendant remains in jail, he will call the attorney many times.

If the defendant remains in jail, he will not get very many visits from his defense attorney. Going to the jail is not pleasant for many lawyers. There are some instances where the defense attorney has to visit the defendant in jail, mostly to have documents signed.

Over the years of my jail visits, there seemed to be a move to keep investigators and lawyers physically away from defendants. We used to be able to sit in a conference room, a small room having a table and three or four metal chairs. I have interviewed inmates in a common area of a cell block, where the cells were located on a terrace overlooking the interviewing area.

This began changing around 2003 when I would go to jail or prison to see an inmate and have to communicate through a glass partition, sliding documents through an opening at the bottom of the glass partition. Guards were always there to watch the interview. Communication then became harder when the only way to talk to the inmate was a closed telephone system, talking on a phone as you looked at the inmate through the glass partition. No documents or papers could be exchanged.

Public Defenders are not second-rate defense attorneys. I have worked with Public Defenders and they can be as effective as private attorneys, but I have seen lazy and corrupt Public Defenders; they seem to become very "chummy" with prosecutors because they see the prosecutors more often than private attorneys.

PROSECUTOR AND BAIL BONDSMAN

Control

Much of this relationship was addressed in <u>Chapter Two- The Prosecutor</u>. The bottom line is that the prosecutor has a lot of control over the bail bondsman, but if the prosecutor wants to have a conviction, he needs the bondsman.

The prosecutor controls the bail bondsman by the following:

The NCIC Decision

Not all bench warrants are put into NCIC. If the prosecutor gets an attitude, or want to protect someone, they will refuse to put the warrant into NCIC. If the fugitive is arrested or has a traffic stop in another jurisdiction, no warrant will appear in NCIC, and the fugitive will not be held, nor will the jurisdiction which issued the bench warrant be notified that their fugitive is in a foreign jail. If the defendant knows his bench warrant is not in NCIC, he can move away and be comfortable that local cops will not know about the warrant on the new guy in town. It is up to the bondsman to follow his leads and find the fugitive.

Many times, a fugitive will resort to criminal activity in another jurisdiction because they are comfortable committing criminal acts, and probably need money because they cannot get a job while they are fugitives.

After a judge agrees for a bench warrant to be issued, the prosecutor will advise law enforcement (or control the computer themselves) whether the fugitive defendant will or will not be extradited.

Being extradited means being transported from a foreign jail to the jurisdiction where the bench warrant was issued.

If the fugitive/defendant is found by law enforcement in a foreign jurisdiction (usually another state), the bondsman will have to go get the fugitive if the prosecutor chooses not to put the bench warrant into NCIC. When it is learned that the fugitive is in another jurisdiction, the bondsman prays that the fugitive is in jail. If the bondsman finds the fugitive/defendant in another state, the bondsman usually packs up and goes to get the fugitive without calling local law enforcement or the prosecutor. There is no need to call anyone for the bondsman to get a fugitive. If the fugitive is far away (over 1,500 miles), the bail bondsman might be able to send a copy of the warrant to the foreign law enforcement agency, showing that the fugitive defendant is filed in NCIC and that the prosecutor will extradite.

The bondsman might be able to get local law enforcement to arrest the fugitive, and that would be great, but that does not happen very often. If a source tells the bondsman that the fugitive is in jail in another state, and the locals did not run the fugitive through NCIC, the locals would not know there was an outstanding warrant. The fugitive could be let out of jail on the current charge and be a fugitive again. That is why it is important for the bondsman to know the NCIC number of each bench warrant.

Informants, sources, and family members might tell the bondsman if the fugitive is in jail in another jurisdiction. That is always a question to be asked when searching for a fugitive.

If the fugitive is in jail, the bondsman needs to determine when the fugitive will be released. A bond hearing might be coming up in the foreign jurisdiction and the defendant needs to be picked up before he leaves the jail. This might take a call from the bondsman to the prosecutor, begging the prosecutor to call the foreign law enforcement or foreign prosecutor and ask that the fugitive be held so the bondsman can pick up the fugitive. Sometimes the jail will hold off processing an inmate for release as a favor for the bondsman to get the fugitive. This will put the burden on the bail bond company to catch the fugitive even if the defendant is being held in another area for a brief time, maybe overnight.

Prosecutor does not want to pay for extradition-

The prosecutor's office will use the excuse that they do not want to spend taxpayer dollars for extradition. There are professional extradition companies which transfer fugitives. Playing the extradition game is another way the prosecutor controls this family member.

Declaring a Defendant as a Fugitive

The defendant might not show up for a roll call. The judge will issue a bench warrant.

The defendant might have violated probation or conditions of the bail bond. This includes not showing up for a scheduled check-in at either the bond company or the probation office. If the defendant has a dirty urine sample when he does his check-in at the probation office, he can be arrested immediately.

The defendant might have been arrested while he was on probation, which is a probation violation. Once the defendant is bonded out on probation violation, he still must visit his probation officer. If the person violated probation and was arrested, he will need a bondsman to get him out of jail on the charge of violation of probation, and more money for the bondsman.

There is a time lapse between the time a person is arrested for violation of probation and the time a decision is made in court that the person did violate probation. The person is arrested, bonded out, and waits for his probation hearing. This means if a person is arrested for probation violation, he will have to go back to court and probably will be found guilty.

The office of probation might contact the bond company if the defendant did not show up for regular probation visits, or if he had a dirty urine sample, both of which violate the probation (again), and a bench warrant will be requested from a judge. This gives the bonding company a head-start in finding the defendant. Even though the probation office can arrest the defendant, the bonding company can usually act faster to arrest the defendant.

If a person violated probation while out on bond, the probation office investigators and the bondsman will both be looking for the defendant. The relationship between the probation office and the bondsman is usually very good because the probation office is swamped with defendants, and violators. Again, the bondsman needs to make sure the new bench warrant is put into NCIC.

The following story will show you how unethical and vindictive prosecutors can be.

I had a fugitive case in South Carolina where the wife of a former highway patrolman was arrested for financial fraud. Both the man and the wife moved to Las Vegas. I found them. The man was working security at a casino. I believe the female was working at a Wal Mart. The female was arrested by Las Vegas police for theft. The police ran the lady's record and saw that she had outstanding warrants in South Carolina, including Failure to Appear. Las Vegas police contacted the local prosecutor, knowing I had made the contact with Las Vegas.

I wanted to hold the defendant for the South Carolina charges. The prosecutor went into the computer system, changed the coding on the computer to reflect that the defendant would not be extradited. The prosecutor then told me to go get the defendant myself or else the bonding company would have to pay the entire amount of the bond. The person in the prosecutor's office who changed the NCIC status was a lawyer, and I recently heard that she is now a dog groomer. She was one of the most corrupt persons I had met.

This was a very dirty prosecutor. This was all about vengeance when I beat the prosecutor on a criminal defense case.

We even asked if Las Vegas could place a hold on the defendant until we could get there. They could not help without the cooperation of the prosecutor. Without the help of the prosecutor, we would have had to go to Las Vegas and spend the time to track down the defendant.

The fugitive was released. The prosecutor did not call the bond due. I was waiting to tell the judge what the prosecutor did, but I never got the chance.

The prosecutor dropped the charges. The prosecutor knew I would have exposed the misconduct. This prosecutor was dirty.

It is very important that the warrant information be put into NCIC, and information must be included that the defendant will be extradited. This helps the bail bond company, but sometimes the prosecutor simply does not care.

The bondsman had better stay current with the status of the incarcerated fugitive. The fugitive could accidentally be released, and the bonding company will again have to look for the fugitive.

There is no pressure on the prosecutor. The prosecutor wants a conviction, but the prosecutor will blame the fact that the defendant remains a fugitive on shoddy work by the bail bond company.

THE PROSECUTOR AND LAW ENFORCEMENT

Arrests, Votes, Convictions

Law enforcement needs arrests. Prosecutors need votes, which means they need convictions.

There is an adage: You cannot make chicken salad from chicken shit. The prosecutor needs solid information from law enforcement to get a conviction or be given enough information to make a conviction stick, even if it means fooling the public, and the defendant.

Law enforcement presents information to a prosecutor to get a warrant. Law enforcement sells the idea of a warrant to the prosecutor when a victim reports the crime to law enforcement. Many times, law enforcement acts as a roadblock to victims because law enforcement has the luxury of making the decision of presenting the case to the prosecutor. Victims of many nonviolent crimes will have to "sell" their case to the law enforcement to get a prosecution.

Arrests and convictions are necessary to show the public that law enforcement is doing their job, allowing the sheriff and prosecutor to continue to be elected. Are there gray areas with respect to the gathering or reporting evidence and an arrest? Of course, there are gray areas. It is blatant abuse and corrupt acts which could, if known by the public, contaminate the case.

Plea Agreements Make Misconduct Disappear

When a defendant takes a plea agreement, the abuse, lies, and criminal activity of a prosecutor and law enforcement is hidden.

The defendant will stand in front of a judge, plead guilty to the charges read, and very little about the process of arresting the defendant will be given. A plea in a high-profile case allows law enforcement and prosecutors the "theater" of the courtroom to make the public think they were so smart to catch the defendant.

I cannot overemphasize the issue of a plea, and the misconduct which is never revealed. Most of the time, when you see a plea, something stinks. The important thing the defendant must do is convince his fellow inmates that he did not "rat out" anyone else to get a plea, which if found out, will get the inmate killed.

Prosecutor and their Investigators do not Generate Evidence.

Law enforcement is the investigative arm of the prosecutor. The prosecutor does hire "investigators" but they rarely generate any original information for the prosecutor. Investigators in the prosecutor office will interview a witness and "prepare" them to testify, and maybe take a statement and deliver subpoenas. The evidence in the prosecutor file comes from law enforcement, not the prosecutor's investigators.

Law Enforcement Knows Prosecutor's File Content

When the prosecutor is served with a Brady Motion, and told to give up evidence (or lack of evidence) against the defendant, the shell game begins.

The only persons who really know what is in the file are the prosecutor and the law enforcement investigator who worked the case. Law enforcement investigators can withhold evidence from the prosecutor which will prove the defendant innocent, and only include circumstantial evidence or manufactured evidence (such as false statements from inmates or snitches). Therefore, it is important that the defendant hire a good PI to find out what is in the file of both the law enforcement and the prosecutor.

If a subpoena is delivered to law enforcement, the law enforcement probably will state that the prosecutor has their file. That is not true; the law enforcement has information and notes which is not given to the prosecutor.

Prosecutor and Law Enforcement Mantra: Quiet

Law enforcement and prosecutors routinely tell informants not to talk to the defense. Several types of leverage can be used against the informants. The difficult part of the defense work is to have an informant help the defense and not fear law enforcement or the prosecutor.

The prosecution witness who is incarcerated or has a criminal record has usually been pressured to give testimony and has been promised a reward. These witnesses could be "jail-house snitches" who are looking to have some of their time reduced. You will always find information about reports of jail house snitches being used to give false testimony.

The best weapon for the defense is a good private investigator; one who is honest and will fight to defend his client

The only way to battle a prosecutor when the defense attorney gets incomplete information as a result of a Brady Motion, is to hire a good PI. The PI might be former law enforcement, and still might be friends with those in the system. Sometimes the PI is not working for the defendant; he is working for the defense attorney, who is working to please the prosecutor. Many PI's "kiss up" to the defense attorney because that is where the PI makes their money.

It takes a very independent (and sometimes crazy) PI to challenge the defense attorney when it is clear that the defendant is getting screwed by both the prosecution and the defense attorney.

The PI will have to generate leads of sources who communicated with law enforcement and find out what is being hidden from the defense. If the defense attorney never confronts the prosecutor or law enforcement, you will know that the fix is in, and the defendant is doomed. The PI can either go with the flow and be quiet or he can confront the defense attorney, law enforcement, and the prosecutor.

I knew some PI's who were weak, sniveling, cowards. I detested those suck-ups. It is not all about the money; it is about battling the dirty guys. The weak PI will become as dirty as any of the other family members and can sabotage a criminal defense.

Pressuring Witnesses

Leverage is used against persons to get them to testify on behalf of the prosecution. A person might be on probation, and a visit from law enforcement might convince them to help the prosecution. People on probation are a wealth of information.

The Prosecutor's Blind Eye

Prosecutors will turn a blind eye to misconduct of law enforcement as long as a conviction is obtained, and the defense does not realize the evidence was bad or the prosecutor committed misconduct. This can be a very slippery slope, and a prosecutor does not want a case to blow up in front of them.

It is more likely that misconduct on the part of the prosecutor will be pointed out by the defense attorney instead of the judge. If the judge points it out, the defense attorney is probably in bed (remember, this is a family) with the prosecutor and has agreed not to object to questionable evidence being presented.

Exposure of Prosecutors

The prosecutor will bear the brunt of law enforcement corruption if the bad evidence is discovered and presented in court. The prosecutor is in open court presenting "evidence" he knows is faulty. If he submits something which has been tainted by law enforcement, the prosecutor will be the one called down because he is the one submitting false evidence. You would think a prosecutor is smart enough to question "evidence" submitted to them by law enforcement in order to obtain a conviction. Sometimes the prosecution thinks they can use   manufactured evidence to intimidate the defense. That does happen. It is rare that a prosecutor will call down a law enforcement officer as long as a conviction can be obtained. It is ultimately up to the prosecutor to present the "evidence." They are family, after all.

Since the prosecutor has absolute immunity in the courtroom, the prosecutor is able to present anything they want; anything.

The prosecutor will simply claim immunity or ignorance, and nothing happens. After the arrest has been made, and the defendant is in jail, the limited/qualified immunity enjoyed by the prosecutor ends. The prosecutor will then become the advocate and has absolute immunity.

Law enforcement has limited immunity, never absolute immunity. Here is where the prosecutor can control and use law enforcement, then use absolute immunity to excuse their misconduct.

Remember the case of the two men in Pottawattamie County, where the police pressured the witnesses to testify against the two men? The limited immunity enjoyed by the police did not excuse them pressuring people into making false statements, but the prosecutor used the statements to prosecute the two men. Even though the prosecutor was involved with the police and had knowledge of the misconduct on the part of the police, this was in the investigative phase of the case, and the prosecutor supposedly had limited immunity. When a witness recanted his statement, telling that he was pressured, the prosecutor basically threw all the blame on law enforcement and took none of the blame. This is finger-pointing at its best.

When the case was settled for millions of dollars, all misconduct was forgotten, and no one got fired. The prosecutors had a delicate task of trying to defend his own behavior, but in order to do that, they had to place all the blame on law enforcement. Law enforcement was not going to accuse the prosecutor of encouraging or collaboration, but it happened. The case settled before the opinion came down from the Supreme Court.

The justices did not get the opportunity to expose the dirty laundry of that part of "the family." The oral argument, noted before, really went after the prosecutor.

The prosecutor and law enforcement have to protect each other in the courtroom, like a big brother defending a younger brother. After all, this is family.

THE PROSECUTOR AND THE DEFENDANT

The Vulnerable Defendant

"It is in this realm in which the prosecutor picks some person whom he dislikes or desires to embarrass or selects some group of unpopular persons and then looks for an offense, that the greatest danger of abuse of prosecuting power lies. It is here that law enforcement becomes personal, and the real crime becomes that of being unpopular with the predominant or governing group, being attached to the wrong political views, or being personally obnoxious to or in the way of the prosecutor himself."[103]

Once you get arrested, the prosecutor owns you, the defendant.

The prosecutor will send law enforcement back to see you and use you as an informant if you cannot make bail, and all you want is to get out of jail. You might have a defense attorney but that does not keep the cops from working with an informant in jail if the cops offer the deal to the informant. They will talk to a defendant even if no attorney is present.

Prosecutors can drop charges for any reason. Sometimes it the result of a direct payoff (like the case I mentioned earlier, when the $20,000 fee to his defense attorney was split with the prosecutor). Sometimes it is in anticipation of future referrals when the prosecutor goes into private practice.

Sometimes charges are dropped as a favor for a friend, or future business.

As Justice Jackson stated, a prosecutor can have an agenda and find probable cause to arrest the most unlikely persons.

It is like an IRS audit; the perception is they will find something if they dig deep enough.

Charges Create Pressure

A prosecutor will threaten a defendant for information or admission by creating a scenario of other charges (many false) which can be made against the defendant.

When the defendant is arrested, the prosecutor can ask for a high bail to "persecute" a defendant into making a deal.

In my book, "Don't Get Arrested in South Carolina", my client was originally charged with Failure to Report a Traffic Accident Having Property Damage in Excess of $1,000. The original bond was set at $250,000. This is more than for a person charged in some murder cases. After my client refused to talk to give a statement or plea to the investigators, he retained an attorney and the bond was reduced to $50,000. The excessive bond was used to pressure my client. The amount remained excessive.

The control of the amount of the bond by the prosecutor will keep the defendant in jail. The defendant is poor, and his family or friends cannot afford to pay the 10 percent of the bond to get the defendant out of jail. The defendant will remain in jail until he gets a trial, or he agrees to enter a plea.

I know prosecutors who get high on pot and cocaine. One prosecutor stole cocaine from the property room, replacing the cocaine with sugar.

It is quite hypocritical for a prosecutor to prosecute a person for doing exactly what the prosecutor does. The defendant will get a deal, and then become the dealer for the prosecutor.

The defendant cannot enter a plea unless he has a lawyer. If he is in jail, he has to wait to be contacted by the prosecutor or by a public defender. If the defendant cannot reach the public defender, nothing gets done. Many times, the defendant will sit in a county jail for quite a while, trying to call the office of the public defender, and having not been assigned one.

The prosecutor controls when to bring a defendant to trial. This delay tactic can be used as leverage against a defendant to keep pressure on him and make him give up information on others. The prosecutor knows that a person will not be brought to trial because the evidence is weak, or there is no evidence, but the person was arrested anyway. This is used as a pressure tactic against a defendant. Many defendants who have extensive records will take a plea just because they are tired of fighting, but part of the plea is giving up information. Being out on bail is restrictive, and the defendant wants to be out from that pressure.

The prosecutor is not supposed to have someone arrested unless the prosecutor plans to bring that person to trial.

Personal Recognizance versus Money Bonds

Keeping the defendant in jail for minor infractions (mostly drug possession related) costs taxpayers tons of money. Personal recognizance bonds (meaning the person can be out on their "word") can be used. These are called "PR" bonds.

Law enforcement does not like a PR bond because this bond does not involve a bail bond company, and if the person does not show up for a roll call, it is up to the law enforcement to find and arrest the defendant, who would then be a fugitive.

These defendants are poor, cannot travel far, have no passports, and pressure put on family members will usually result in a quick capture if they violate the bond. Sometimes defendants do not have transportation to get from court to their home.

There is a movement to allow drug users and other non-violent, low level offenders, to have low or no bail. They can get out on a PR Bond (personal recognizance), meaning it is up to them to go to court, or they will be arrested for Failure to Show. This would impact the bail bond industry, reduce the prison population, and reduce the cost of housing people who just want to get high and not hurt anyone.

Jail is a Business, and Prosecutors Profit

Tax dollars are doled out to communities based upon the number of inmates. Many jails and prisons now are operated by "prison companies" and not by local law enforcement. The more inmates, the more money, and everyone except the defendant benefits. Jobs are created, independent contractors within the prison industry make money, and more money is allocated to the prosecutor and public defender office.

Keeping the defendant in jail is good business. There is a better chance of getting a guilty plea from the defendant if the defendant is in jail.

As I mentioned before, if the defendant has money, they are treated differently. If the defendant has lots of money, he can put up property as security for a bond, and if he is found not guilty, he gets the lien taken off his property, and the bond cost him nothing. Other defendants pay the ten percent and do not get a refund. That is no fair to poor people.

Defense attorneys who are close friends with prosecutors pay the prosecutors with cash from the retainer paid to the defense attorney. This is done more often on a local level.

The prosecutor who goes into private practice will benefit from a "dirty plea" made for a defendant. The defendant will refer his friends to this former prosecutor, knowing that the former prosecutor will get a deal done as a private attorney.

If the sentence is mandatory, the defendant will want to negotiate a lesser charge instead of dropping a charge in order to get a shorter prison time. The defendant will have to play the game, and "information" and "cooperation" are the tools used by the defendant to help the defendant.

THE PROSECUTOR AND DEFENSE ATTORNEY

Power and Money

"Prosecutors take the job to gain power to get money; defense attorneys take the job to get the money to gain power."

Prosecutors are judged by defendant convictions. That is simple. The law enforcement furnishes defendants to the prosecutor to obtain a conviction, after the defense attorney has been paid by the defendant. These family members need each other, but some things about the relationship between the prosecutor and defense attorney are not as they seem.

Many times, a defense attorney has been a prosecutor. Fewer times will an attorney in private practice ever go to get a job as a prosecutor because in private practice, the defense attorneys defend defendants and will have a bad taste in their mouth for prosecution.

If an attorney chooses to practice criminal defense straight out of law school, it is rare that he becomes a prosccutor. It is rare that a person changes from becoming a public defender to a prosecutor. It is in the blood; some like to defend and some like to prosecute. Some want the power of a prosecutor. Some like the good feeling of defending a person, and the money.

It is like a board game; the prosecutor and defense attorney move the pieces around the board, and the roll of the dice dictates the next move. Defendants are the pieces.

The other members of the family have to sit back and watch the prosecutor and the defense attorney ultimately control the outcome of the case. Law enforcement can give evidence, the bondsman can

make sure the defendant is in court, the defendant can be left in the dark with respect to what is being done, but these other three family members are helpless when a deal is made with the prosecutor and defense attorneys.

The prosecutor and the defense attorney see the other three family members as a means to an end; financial gain and power. Both need other members of the family, but it is as though the prosecutor is the father and the defense attorney is the mother.

Both are lawyers. Both look down upon the other family members because they are "not lawyers" and not as smart as the lawyers. The prosecutor and defense attorney might have grown up in the same city, gone to the same college, attend the same church, or were classmates in law school. Book smarts does not always evolve into street smarts, or how to deal with people on a personal manner, but the prosecutor and defense attorney let the other members furnish the street smarts.

There are other connections to be made between these lawyer family members. Wives could be friends. Secrets are known (drug use and infidelity are biggies). If a defense attorney has a reputation of being able to get deals, the defendant will tell his friends. If the prosecutor is not being paid enough under the table to make a difference in his life, he waits for the day he can become a defense attorney and use the knowledge and leverage to make the money to gain the power on the outside.

Prosecutors know it is against the law for a defendant to use the rewards of his criminal activity to pay for the defense attorney. The prosecutor could have assets of the defendant held from the defendant, but these high-profile defendants have money in other places to pay the defense attorney.

Defense attorneys who have the connection with the prosecutor are not going to embarrass a prosecutor in the courtroom or to the press. There are some exceptions (Gerry Spence, F. Lee Bailey, and other aggressive defense attorneys) but the local defense attorney is usually not going to attack a prosecutor for misconduct. This could be done on appeal by a different attorney, and the appeal is generated by the defendant.

A defense attorney can make a deal with the prosecutor, outside law enforcement, to have the defendant become an informant. The defense attorney can take a statement from   his client, the defendant, and offer it up to the prosecutor. This gives the defendant a bit of credibility with law enforcement, or maybe irritates law enforcement a little because law enforcement was not able to extract the information from the defendant. This keeps the deal between the prosecutor and the defense attorney. Cutting law enforcement out of the loop really makes law enforcement angry, and the defendant will play that game, communicating with prosecutor investigators instead of law enforcement.

The friends of the defendant know that if charges are dropped or reduced greatly, the defendant became an informant. Criminals know that they are going to have to tell something on somebody at some time.

Almost all defendants have ratted out someone for something. This is a very dangerous business, and the prosecutor is still in charge.

It is expected that the prosecutor will use the defendant as a tool to solve more facets of a crime, such as co-conspirators, or supplying information that law enforcement did not have. Arrest one person involved in the crime and you probably will find out who else was involved.

THE BAIL BONDSMAN AND LAW ENFORCEMENT

Similar Objectives, Personal Issues

After the bench warrant is issued (the judge is sitting on the "bench" orders a warrant, thus a "bench warrant"), the prosecutor who is seated next to the judge, takes the list of names back to the prosecutor's office to have warrants written. The prosecutor takes the completed bench warrant to the judge, and the judge signs the warrant (which can take a few days). The warrant information is sent to the law enforcement agency which arrested the defendant. Usually the warrant information is sent to the county sheriff to be put into their computer system.

As I mentioned earlier, the prosecutor does have a hand in having the warrant put into the computer, and into the NCIC system. The prosecutor in South Carolina removed a warrant from NCIC for personal reasons.

The sticky part of the relationship between law enforcement and bail bonding is egos. Some law enforcement officers look at bondsmen as the whores of the legal system, making tons of money off arrested defendants, and basically making more money than the lowly law enforcement agent. There is some financial jealousy, which can spill over in a lack of cooperation. Bondsmen can make a good living, but it is the bail bond company owner making the big bucks, not the hired bondsman.

Most law enforcement officers are helpful and cooperative with bondsman. Sometimes it all boils down to that dreaded ego. If the bondsman is disrespectful, he will get no cooperation.

The bondsman NEEDS law enforcement. Some law enforcement will tell the bondsman that the fugitive is not the problem of law enforcement, and the bondsman will get little or no cooperation from law enforcement. Law enforcement knows that the bondsman is going after the fugitive for a charge of Failure to Appear, which is low priority to law enforcement.

If the bondsman can find law enforcement officers who are adamant about arresting the fugitives, and the bondsman does not waste the time of law enforcement personnel, law enforcement can be the saving grace, and each family member can help one another.

There were times when a fugitive was holed up in a house and we could not get him out. We contacted law enforcement, showed the warrant, and law enforcement would assist by bringing in more people to help. This was great, and it always helps for a bail bondsman to have that good relationship.

There were times when family members of fugitives told us that the fugitive was in jail in another county. The bondsman would call that county, confirm that the fugitive was in jail, and let the jailer know that the defendant has a current warrant for failure to appear. You would think that after a fugitive was arrested in another jurisdiction that the record of an outstanding warrant would show up. This goes back to the prosecutor, and maybe the local law enforcement, to put the correct information into the computer, and put the warrant into NCIC. If the information is not put into NCIC, the other jurisdiction has no way of confirming that the person in their jail has an outstanding warrant for failure to appear.

If a defendant is scheduled to be released very soon, sometimes the jail can be convinced to hold that person for the bondsman to appear and get the fugitive and return him to the original jurisdiction. (Being arrested is a violation of the bond, so the defendant can be arrested and taken back to the original jail just because he was arrested while out on bond.)

If the defendant is serving some time for the crime committed in the other jurisdiction, the bondsman will have to keep up with the date of release and be at the jail when the defendant is released.

In all cases, the bondsman must create a good relationship with law enforcement, correction officers, jailers, and other bondsman. Egos can cost all persons a lot of money.

There are times when the bail bondsman has a strong lead that takes him to another jurisdiction. Most times the bondsman will contact the police agency in the area where the lead takes the bondsman. There are advantages of having a bondsman pick up fugitives in a foreign jurisdiction, and the cops there are open to the bondsman.

Some of the advantages of having bail bondsmen in the area are no local cops will be injured, local paperwork; no warrants or reports to submit. Fugitives usually commit criminal acts to survive, wherever they live. Local cops want fugitive out of their area.

Fugitives have signed away their rights, so bondsmen just can enter a residence without a warrant. The bondsman can get away with more indiscreet acts than can law enforcement. If the bondsman strokes the ego of law enforcement, things can go very well.

THE BAIL BONDSMAN AND DEFENDANT

The Pre-Arranged Marriage

In February of 2004 a bail bond company became my client. I was hired to find their missing defendants, known as fugitives. The list of fugitives was printed out on over 3 sheets of paper, in landscape fashion. The work began as one phone call at a time. Databases had started being used for the prior 6 years or more by PI's and they were helpful, but nothing beats getting a person on the phone, or making a visit to a person, and getting information. It is an art, a talent. I had that talent. I could tell who did and did not have that intuitive talent. It is called social engineering.

The first take-down was a defendant who was the son of a bail bondsman. This person had been in prison for a violent crime and was on bond for violating parole. I believe he missed probation meetings, and bench warrant was issued. I had not studied his case much, but the owner of the bonding company was well aware of the defendant, and the fact that he had not been seen in a while. I rode with another bondsman as sources were questioned, one being a hamburger cook at a local dirty hole in the wall. The date was April 15, 2004. I was 50 years old, thinking I was too old for this.

The information was hot. Our boy was working at a little barbeque hut, located on a major highway just north of town. A source could identify the defendant, so he (short, black, raggedy clothes) and I (white, stocky build, and a little taller) walk to the window to get barbecue. The source recognized the fugitive, cooking barbecue.

The source made a motion to the rest of the crew (3 others hiding in cars) and the barbeque hut was approached.

One of the others, posing as a bondsman, was the most crazy, aggressive, methamphetamine and cocaine addict you will ever meet. The addict was basically picking up extra money from the bonding company.

The addict charged the fugitive and hit him high, knocking him to the floor of the barbecue hut. The owner of the bonding company yelled, "Get in there, Jim" so I dove in and grabbed his legs.

The defendant was kicking like crazy. Another bondsman (John) was standing over me. I yelled at John, "get the chains" so we could wrap up his legs. The chains were knotted, and John was trying to untangle the leg chains. It was probably only a minute, but it seemed a lot longer before John could get the chains unknotted and jump in to secure the fugitive's legs, all the while the other bondsman was fighting with the fugitive face to face.

Welcome to fugitive apprehension.

In 18 months, I only had maybe 5 big fights. I was very good at calming a person down, especially when they thought I was a crazy ass white man. I would arrest them, give them food, drink, smokes, and treat them well.

It is amazing to see the persons who have the common sense and intellect of the bail bondsman. These people can connect the dots; it is amazing to see the social skills they have to have in order to find a fleeing defendant. They are not buffoons.

The attitude toward most defendants by the bondsman is one of not being judgmental. It is not just the fact that the bondsman is happy to be paid, and that the defendant is happy to be out of jail. Most bondsmen genuinely want the defendant to go to court.

It is almost a contradiction because the bondsman makes his money on people who make bad decisions and get caught.

The atmosphere in the bonding office was very pleasant when defendants came in for their monthly check in. Most laugh at the fact that they "messed up" and find no stigma attached to having a record.

When a defendant becomes a fugitive, the bondsman will make a presence in the neighborhood. Friends and neighbors will not like this, especially in a low-income housing area. People in the hood know the cops and the bondsman. Even though most people don't really care, many get nervous when bondsmen and police stay in their area. This added attention to the area is a ploy used by the bondsman and law enforcement to find the defendant by having someone reveal the location of the defendant. This is called making the defendant "hot." The defendant cannot go home. The defendant has to sleep on the couch of friends, but then the friends turn him out. The friends do not want the added police and bondsmen present in the area. The bondsman will get a call at the office to tell the bondsman where to find the defendant. That happens all the time.

The defendant would much rather be picked up by the bondsman than by law enforcement even though the bondsman has fewer rules.

Law enforcement is very aware of the scrutiny they face by using force to capture a defendant. The bondsmen have no cameras and have little patience with foolishness. If the defendant was nice, I would buy him a drink; give him some cigarettes to smoke on the way to jail, and even food.

Once I allowed a fleeing defendant to finish a joint (marijuana) he was smoking on his back porch. He saw me parking a big Chevrolet Suburban near his apartment, and I parked to watch him get high before I took him in. He walked to me without me having to get out of my vehicle.

If you want to fight, you can create the atmosphere for a fight. The fleeing defendant is tired. He has been running. He has had to be on guard every minute. The words a fleeing defendant understands are, "It's time." It is time to go to jail and get this behind you. If the defendant is upset or angry, they usually calm down before getting to jail.

Remember, the bondsmen want the business, and referrals are a part of the business. If you treat the defendant well, he will refer his friends to you, and believe me, if the defendant is committing crimes, so are his friends.

Defendants also identify "dirty cops" so the bondsman will be aware who and who not to trust.

THE BAIL BONDSMAN AND DEFENSE ATTORNEY

Who Trusts Who?

The first thing a person who has been arrested wants is to get out of jail.

The first person he calls from jail will be either a family member or a bail bond company.

The bail bond company will call the family member and have them come to the office to sign a bond and get their relative out of jail.

The sooner the defendant can get out of jail, the sooner he can get to an attorney.

If the arrested person is lucky enough to have an attorney present at the bond hearing (which can be 24 hours after being arrested), the bond amount is announced, and the defense attorney can make arguments to reduce the bail. The defense attorney will need to be paid by a family member before going to a bond hearing to argue the bond.

If the arrested person or a family member calls the bail bond company before the bond hearing, the bail bond company has to wait for the bail amount to be announced before finishing the paperwork. Bail bond companies have access to databases which show the amount of the person's bail. If the bail is high, somehow the family members must hire an attorney for the arrested man, or the arrested man can call the attorney from jail and ask the defense attorney to approach the judge to lower the bail. The defense attorney is not going to a bond hearing for free.

This is where the relationship between the bail bondsman and the defense attorney is important. Neither the defense attorney nor the bail bond companies are legally supposed to give referrals to each other, but it happens because the arrested person will ask one to make a referral for the other. If an arrested person previously used a bail bond company, he will usually call the same one to get out of jail.

The bondsman can make the referral of a defense attorney to a family member of the arrested suspect, but that referral is never discussed, and the bondsman's name will not be used regarding the defense attorney.

If an arrested person, now a defendant, fails to appear in any court proceeding, the bondsman will have to go find the defendant. The bondsman might call the defense attorney to see if the defense attorney has any information which will help capture the defendant/fugitive.

The defense attorney knows the bondsman can help "line his pockets" so the bondsman ultimately has the upper hand in this relationship. It can become complicated if the defendant has to choose where his money is going to be spent: the bondsman has a fee and the defense attorney has a fee. If the bond is high, the bond company might have to finance some of the fee for the defendant to get a defense attorney.

LAW ENFORCEMENT AND THE DEFENDANT

A Multi-Faceted Relationship

This is a very interesting relationship. Some people think that law enforcement officers are criminals wearing badges. I would not go so far as to say that, but my experience is that there is a reason some people draw that conclusion. Law enforcement is exposed to more temptation to become criminals than most other professions, and good people will turn bad.

There are times when the simple arrest of a suspect will cause the suspect to lose his job. Just the threat of losing a job will make a person cooperate with law enforcement.

Once a person becomes a defendant, then convicted, the defendant usually gets probation rather than a sentence to be served in jail or prison. People who are on probation are the information whores for law enforcement. Probation can be revoked if the defendant has a run in with law enforcement, and the defendant will be back in jail for probation violation. Cooperating with the cops might be a condition of probation, and cops squeeze very hard to get information and cooperation.

The informant is usually identified as either working "for the cops" or working "with the cops."

If you are working with the cops, you would usually not have a record and are not on probation. You are just passing along information.

If you are working <u>for</u> the cops, you are doing it to be paid or you are under pressure. You might have a record, be on probation, or the cops are aware of your criminal activity but will look away if you help the cops when they ask.

As I said before, most repeat criminals look at jail as a cost of doing business. They choose to continue the criminal business and pay the cost. That is the reason for repeat offenders; the defendant is in the same business as last time he was arrested. He knows no other way to make fast money, or any money.

One dirty little secret is the "shakedown" of a former defendant or informant by law enforcement. As mentioned before, the law enforcement will be aware of criminal activity by the defendant and take either money or spoils of the crime (usually drugs).

The essay written by Ms. Alexandra Natapoff, <u>Snitching: Criminal Informants and the Erosion of American Justice,</u> does give a good overview of the subject of informants. Her position is, as the title states, having informants does nothing to promote justice. As a veteran on the street, needing informants to solve problems and find people, I know the importance of informants. I disagree that informants are part of the erosion of American justice; informants solve crimes, almost all crimes.

The biggest part of the erosion of the American justice system is corrupt prosecutors and corrupt law enforcement, not the use of informants.

Do law enforcement officers allow informants to commit crimes in order to catch other people? Yes, they do. Do some informants have to pay their law enforcement handler proceeds of illegal activity?

Yes, they do. Any crime you can think of that can be excused can be committed by an informant and overlooked by law enforcement. If law enforcement overlooks things, the prosecutor never comes into the picture unless the informant "rats out" a dirty cop.

Professor Natapoff feels the informants are being rewarded by having their crimes forgiven. My answer to that is you cannot prosecute all crimes. Like a hospital, cops use a triage method to determine who they want to get, and if it takes allowing an informant to commit a crime to get a certain person, it will happen.

Natapoff stated that secret deals, not being transparent, are the most "problematic."[104]

Well, that is the way it happens. Cops do not talk to informants on the courthouse steps; they talk privately. Yes, the promises are not heard, and the secret time and discussions between law enforcement and the informant is supposed to remain secret.

Law enforcement will work on a criminal defendant to get him to become an informant, meaning being "flipped." Some information never comes to light because the defendant will take the plea, based upon informant information. Friends of the defendant know the defendant had to give up some information to get probation, but the defendant will always deny he gave any information. Yeah, yeah, yeah.

Natapoff proposes some reform to the secretiveness of the relationship between law enforcement and informants. I do not see that happening. That prospect is short sighted and a bit like living on Sunny Brook Farm.

Do cops get compromised by informants? Yes, they do. Look at Whitey Bulger and his FBI handler, Connolly. It happens more than you know. Who is going to arrest the informant? Who is going to arrest the cop? Do cops sell drugs? Yes, they do.

Do cops allow a criminal enterprise to continue, and be paid to not report it? I personally know of these incidents.

As stated before, there are guidelines which allow informants to commit crimes.

According to Ms. Natapoff:

Most importantly, using informants entails the official toleration of crime, both past and present. By their nature, informant deals require that law enforcement ignore or reduce liability for an informant's past misdeeds. Although drug defendants famously cooperate, no class of offenders is off-limits": snitching can reduce or eliminate liability for crimes as diverse as kidnapping, arson, gambling, and murder.

As part of the process of gathering information, active informants necessarily continue to engage in criminal activity. Drug informants, of example, are routinely authorizes to buy, sell, and even use drugs in pursuit of targets. More broadly, U.S. Department of Justice guidelines expressly contemplate ongoing informant criminality with two tiers of "Otherwise Illegal Activity" that can be authorized by the handler. Tier 1 Otherwise Illegal Activity includes violent crimes committed by someone other than the informant, official corruption, theft, and the manufacture or distribution of drugs, including the provision of drugs with no expectation of recovering them. Tier 2 activity includes all other criminal offenses. [105]

Ms. Natapoff was referring to the Department of Justice Guidelines Regarding the Use of Confidential Informants (January 8, 2001).

The informant has to earn his permission to commit crime, but to the informant, it is only a cost of doing business. If law enforcement wants that particular person to give up sensitive information, law enforcement will have to pay to get the information.

Informants can help solve crimes that would never have been solved. They are vital to the criminal justice family.

Another cost of doing business, as an informant, is getting caught being an informant. Criminals on the street know cops use informants. The criminals know many cops are bad, and they choose which cops are safe to conduct business. But, if an informant is revealed and is out on the street, he is a dead man.

Here are two short stories, one about a shakedown, and one about an informant.

One day I happened to be in the office of the bail bonding company. A young man came in. I looked at his paperwork, seeing the charge was cocaine possession, and I asked him how he got popped.

The defendant was driving in a rural town, and a local town policeman noticed a brake light was out on the defendant's car. The defendant was pulled over, smelling of pot, and gave consent to search the car. I saw the charge of the amount of drugs and cash he was accused of having in his car.

I asked him how much drugs the cops found in his car. The difference was about a third; the cops took a third of the drugs, and only reported the defendant having about half the cash (reported about five thousand dollars in cash). The reduction in the amount of drugs lessened the drug charge for the defendant, and put a stash of drugs in the cop's pocket. It was as if the cops were doing the defendant a favor. It was a combination arrest/shakedown.

Years later, a former law enforcement friend told me how an elected state official was arrested. The arrest was very public and cost the man his state position. This was huge news in the state.

The elected official had been arrested for possession of cocaine, and possession with intent to distribute. It was a big mess. Here is what I was told by an investigator on the case. This elected official used cocaine, and entertained friends at his home on a regular basis. As the friends were being entertained, cocaine was freely given to these friends. Alcohol was also furnished at the gatherings.

One of the regular partygoers was stopped in his car after leaving the home of the elected state official. The party goer was drunk when he left the party. As the driver was being arrested, he told the police that he had information to give, and he made a deal to turn in the elected official. When the elected official was arrested, he had more cocaine than normally kept for personal consumption. The elected official was charged with trafficking cocaine. I believe it eventually came out that the official was not trafficking.

He was giving it away. The official did some time, and the DUI rat was not charged with the DUI.

The DUI guy was not a very good friend.

LAW ENFORCEMENT AND THE DEFENSE ATTORNEY

Contempt, and the Revolving Door

Law enforcement is to the prosecutor as the defendant is to the defense attorney: the prosecutor protects law enforcement and their testimony, and the defense attorney defends the defendant. The defense attorney grills law enforcement on the witness stand, and the prosecutor grills the defendant. The deal makers are the prosecutor and the defense attorney. No deals are done with the defendant or law enforcement.

Law enforcement and defense attorneys are as much, or more, enemies as the defense attorney and the prosecutor. These family members know the dirt on each other and are not afraid to use that leverage. The defense attorney will not push back very hard on a prosecutor because the defense attorney is intent upon attacking the evidence presented by law enforcement. The prosecutor does not create the evidence; law enforcement creates the evidence; thus, the defense attorney initially attacks law enforcement.

The defense attorney will put law enforcement on the witness stand to reveal mistakes and willful incorrect evidence being presented. Defense attorneys get a better reaction from discrediting law enforcement than they do trying to convince a judge that the prosecutor did something wrong. Jurors cannot understand the legalities of prosecutorial misconduct as easily as they can a dirty cop.

Expert witnesses put up by the prosecution are there to validate evidence gathered by law enforcement and prosecutors.

Expert witnesses give their "interpretation" of the evidence. It is there that the defense attorney must attack the validity of the evidence or the gathering and storing of the evidence. Again, this is the defense attorney attacking law enforcement. Professional witnesses are whores of the court system.

Many expert witnesses testify for a living, and work for either prosecution or defense. These "hired guns" say what they are paid to say, either for law enforcement or the defense attorneys, and get paid. Remember the lady expert witness who was found to have falsified evidence concerning the boot of a defendant? Remember the man who falsified evidence of the examination of ricin contamination? This is a gender-neutral issue: expert witnesses are men and women, and many will be paid to say what they need to say.

The defense attorney will be attacking the procedures of law enforcement before the results were given to the expert, then the defense attorney will attack the expert for not admitting that the law enforcement procedures were compromised or lacked credibility.

The feeling from law enforcement toward defense attorneys is just as ugly. The defense attorneys are making the big bucks, defending a bunch of criminals, who law enforcement risked injury or life to arrest, and law enforcement has little regard for the defense attorneys. "The defense attorneys just put the scum back on the street."

The defense attorneys must make deals with the prosecutor, not law enforcement. This really irritates law enforcement.

When law enforcement officers risk their lives to arrest a person, law enforcement wants this defendant prosecuted.

Law enforcement does not want to see a deal made with the prosecutor in which compromises the work performed by law enforcement. The deal is made, a suspended sentence is given, and the defendant smiles at law enforcement as he walks out the courtroom.

If a defense attorney received inadequate records from the prosecutor as a result of filing a Brady Motion, law enforcement knows what was held back. Law enforcement furnished all investigative information to the prosecutor, and the defense attorney can reveal a violation of a Brady Motion by questioning law enforcement about their reports. The defense attorney will make it known that the reports were not given to the defense as the prosecutor was supposed to do. Here is where the defense attorney can make law enforcement expose the prosecutor as hiding evidence; here is where a good defense attorney can use law enforcement as a tool to attack the prosecutor.

Law enforcement will then cover-up for the prosecutor, and make sure the favorable evidence is not found by the defense. Within the Brady violation cases discussed in this book, there was always a representative of law enforcement who knew there were withheld documents. I did not see law enforcement mentioned in the rulings from the Supreme Court; most or all of the attention was aimed toward the prosecutor.

When a person is arrested, there will always be one member of the criminal justice family who will not be happy in the end: this unhappy family member will usually be law enforcement.

J

THE DEFENDANT AND THE DEFENSE ATTORNEY

Surprises

Surprises are nightmares to a defense attorney.

Defendants answer questions from their attorneys, but it is hard to get all the truth from a defendant.

Defense attorneys will tell you, flat out, that defendants will lie. This makes it terribly hard to defend a person, especially when a surprise comes up in the courtroom.

There are instances when defendants get an attorney who is not experienced enough to try the criminal case. Many people criticize public defenders, as though they are the most stupid of the defense attorneys. That is not the case. I did defense work for the office of a public defender in the mid 1990's and found the attorneys to be very capable for the most part. Most were not very aggressive, and a bit too chummy with the prosecutor's office.

I hate to see a criminal conviction overturned because of inadequate defense representation. The defense attorney knows when he has lost control of the case, and if the attorney is a public defender, he has help at the next desk in his office. A defense attorney has to know how to read the evidence and interpret the evidence. The best defense attorney does not need to know all the right answers; he just needs to know the right questions. A good PI can connect dots of contradiction faster than most attorneys.

I have seen some great defense attorneys, having spent upwards to a full week or more in court, every day, at the defense table.

One case involved a man who made moonshine; 300 gallons a week. The defendant told me he was paying bribes to a law enforcement officer, and the law enforcement officer put up the money to get the illegal liquor operation up and running.

I investigated the law enforcement officer and had much dirt on him. I had a witness, who worked for a different law enforcement agency, lunge at me from across a table because I humiliated him in front of a bunch of people. He deserved it. The defense attorney, Dennis Bolt, grilled the law enforcement witnesses unmercifully. Dennis and I did well together. Our man was found not guilty. Dennis believed in the defendant and did one of the best defense jobs I ever saw.

One of the keys to having a good defense is having the defense attorney, the defendant, and the PI all on the same page. The PI will run interference with law enforcement as the defense attorney runs interference with the prosecutor. If law enforcement starts complaining that a PI is causing trouble, he will complain to the prosecutor, who will contact the defense attorney. All I had to do was plant a seed of mistrust in the minds of either law enforcement or a prosecutor, and I was effective.

The most frustrating situation is when a defendant trusts the PI, who is working hard for the defendant, the PI has information to help the defendant, and the defendant sees that his attorney, the defense attorney, is not being proactive enough to attack the evidence put forth by law enforcement, and/or go after the prosecutor. The defendant will lose trust in the defense attorney, and the PI is left to keep his mouth shut.

If the PI confronts the defense attorney and makes an accusation that the defense attorney is not honestly representing the client, the PI will lose the defense attorney as a client.

The defendant begins to trust the PI more than the defense attorney.

Been there, done that.

It looks like we are back to money, again.

I have seen half-assed, suck-up, weak, corrupt, piss-ant, persons who get licensed as a PI. They have no original thoughts, and simply do what the defense attorney tells them to do. The PI will have little contact with the defendant. A good PI can and should be able to interrogate with a defendant as well or better than an attorney, simply because most PI's have been in the street and can pick up on subtle clues and references made by the defendant and the people around the defendant. It is always easier for the defense attorney to get a report of a matter from the PI than having to listen to the ramblings of a defendant.

As a defense attorney, being civil with prosecution is one thing, but the prosecutor is the enemy. The defense attorney must attack for his client, and that means attacking law enforcement and the prosecutor.

The worst thing that can happen to a defendant is to have his lawyer willfully fail to represent him in adequate manner and convince the defendant to take a plea that should not be taken. I saw that happen recently when a defendant took a plea which was recommended by his defense attorney. It was later learned that the defense attorney had submitted the Brady Motion, and the defendant never saw the evidence, including alleged victim statements. The defendant was not given the opportunity to defend himself. The defense attorney was paid over $50,000 on the case and refused to discuss the case. The defendant is now a prisoner and will have to make a motion to get the Brady material while he is in prison.

Some defendants, like the one above, are expendable throwaway clients to the Defense attorneys.

Defense attorney can see dollar signs, knowing they have a bit of leverage and friends at the prosecutor's office to make the sentence a bit lighter, and that costs money that will be paid by the defendant.

If the defense attorney is good, the prosecutor will not want to face him in court. That is when you know the defense attorney is doing his job.

If the defense attorney is corrupt, he will allow his client to go to prison and know the defendant will not see the defense attorney for years.

No conscience is necessary, just a law degree.

EPILOGUE

The criminal justice family is headed by the prosecutor, as a parent would be the head of the family. Law enforcement, defense attorneys, defendants, and bondsmen, are simply the siblings. The parent has the last word. This is the criminal justice system in the United States.

The siblings all want to gain the favor of the head of the family and will battle each other to gain this favor. Dirty deals are made, which amount to incest within the system. Few will battle the head of the family, because they know at some time, they will have to make deals again, and the incest cycle begins again.

Joining the criminal justice family is a big decision. The defendant is the only member of the family who does not initially willingly join the family. Some defendants become a member of the family and become rewarded for contributing to the family. Initially, most of the other family members probably join the family for ethically pure reasons; wanting to defend poor defendants, rid the streets of criminals, put bad people in prison, or enjoy the thrill of the hunt by catching fleeing fugitives. Most of the family members join the family without knowing what you have read in this book. Would they join the family if they knew the corruption of the family members? The answer is yes; only if they were inherently corrupt.

Welcome to the criminal justice family.

ENDNOTES

1.

Russell, Jason, *Look at How Many Pages are in the Federal Tax Code.Washington Examiner.*
,http://www.washingtonexaminer.com/look-at-how-many-pages-are-in-the-federal-tax-code/article/2563032
Assessed April 14, 2106

2.

Officer Down Memorial Page, https://www.odmp.org/agency/3962-united-states-department-of-the-treasury-internal-revenue-service-criminal-investigation-us-government
Accessed April 14, 2016

3.

Robert H. Jackson
https://www.justice.gov/sites/default/files/ag/legacy/2011/09/16/04-01-1940.pdf
Accessed March 26, 2016

4.

https://www.roberthjackson.org/article/robert-h-jackson-biography/
Accessed March 16, 2016

5.

Bennett L. Gershman, The Prosecutor's Duty to Truth, 14 Geo. J. Legal Ethics 309 (2001) http://digitalcommons.pace.edu/lawfaculty/128/.
Berger v. United States, 295 US 78,88 (1935)
Accessed March 17, 2016

6.

John Paul Stevens,
http://www.supremecourt.gov/publicinfo/speeches/Equal%20Justice%20Init%20Dinner%20(1606_001).pdf
Accessed March 22, 2016

7.
John Paul Stevens
http://www.supremecourt.gov/publicinfo/speeches/Equal%20Justice%20
Init%20Dinner%20(1606_001).pdf
Accessed March 22, 2016

8.
Wechler, Robert. *The Special Responsibilities of Prosecutors- and Other Local Government Attorneys.* http://www.cityethics.org/node/460
Accessed April 1, 2016

9.
Margaret Z. Johns, *Reconsidering Absolute Prosecutorial Immunity*,
2005 BYU L. Rev. 53 (2005)
http://digitalcommons.law.byu.edu/lawreview/vol2005/iss1/2
Accessed March 24, 2016

10.
Cornell Law
https://www.law.cornell.edu/supct/html/91-7849.ZO.html
Accessed April 9, 2016

11.
Cornell Law
https://www.law.cornell.edu/supct/html/91-7849.ZO.html
Accessed April 9, 2016

12.
Margaret Z. Johns, *Reconsidering Absolute Prosecutorial Immunity*,
2005 BYU L. Rev. 53 (2005)
http://digitalcommons.law.byu.edu/lawreview/vol2005/iss1/2
Accessed March 24, 2016

13.
Margaret Z. Johns, *Reconsidering Absolute Prosecutorial Immunity*,
2005 BYU L. Rev. 53 (2005)
http://digitalcommons.law.byu.edu/lawreview/vol2005/iss1/2
Accessed March 24, 2016

14.

David Keenan, Deborah Jane Cooper, David Lebowitz & Tamar Lerer, The Myth of Prosecutorial Accountability After Connick v. Thompson: Why Existing Professional Responsibility Measures Cannot Protect Against Prosecutorial Misconduct, 121 Yale L.J. Online 203 (2011), http://yalelawjournal.org/forum/the-myth-of-prosecutorial-accountability-after-connick-v-thompson-why-existing-professional-responsibility-measures-cannot-protect-against-prosecutorial-misconduct Accessed March 16, 2016

15.

Margaret Z. Johns, *Reconsidering Absolute Prosecutorial Immunity*, 2005 BYU L. Rev. 53 (2005) http://digitalcommons.law.byu.edu/lawreview/vol2005/iss1/2 Accessed March 24, 2016

16.

Margaret Z. Johns, Margaret Z. Johns, *Reconsidering Absolute Prosecutorial Immunity*, 2005 BYU L. Rev. 53 (2005) http://digitalcommons.law.byu.edu/lawreview/vol2005/iss1/2 Accessed March 24, 2016

17.

Margaret Z. Johns, *Reconsidering Absolute Prosecutorial Immunity*, 2005 BYU L. Rev. 53 (2005) http://digitalcommons.law.byu.edu/lawreview/vol2005/iss1/2 Accessed March 24, 2016

18.

Margaret Z. Johns, Margaret Z. Johns, *Reconsidering Absolute Prosecutorial Immunity*, 2005 BYU L. Rev. 53 (2005) http://digitalcommons.law.byu.edu/lawreview/vol2005/iss1/2 Accessed March 24, 2016

19.

Margaret Z. Johns, Margaret Z. Johns, *Reconsidering Absolute Prosecutorial Immunity*, 2005 BYU L. Rev. 53 (2005) http://digitalcommons.law.byu.edu/lawreview/vol2005/iss1/2 Accessed March 24, 2016

20.

Margaret Z. Johns, Margaret Z. Johns, *Reconsidering Absolute Prosecutorial Immunity*, 2005 BYU L. Rev. 53 (2005)http://digitalcommons.law.byu.edu/lawreview/vol2005/iss1/2 Accessed March 24, 2016

21.

Margaret Z. Johns, Margaret Z. Johns, *Reconsidering Absolute Prosecutorial Immunity*, 2005 BYU L. Rev. 53 (2005) http://digitalcommons.law.byu.edu/lawreview/vol2005/iss1/2 Accessed March 24, 2016

22.

Margaret Z. Johns, Margaret Z. Johns, *Reconsidering Absolute Prosecutorial Immunity*, 2005 BYU L. Rev. 53 (2005) http://digitalcommons.law.byu.edu/lawreview/vol2005/iss1/2 Accessed March 24, 2016

23.

John Paul Stevens http://www.supremecourt.gov/publicinfo/speeches/Equal%20Justice%20 Init%20Dinner%20(1606_001).pdf Accessed March 22, 2016

24.

John Paul Stevens http://www.supremecourt.gov/publicinfo/speeches/Equal%20Justice%20 Init%20Dinner%20(1606_001).pdf Accessed March 22, 2016

25.

Bloomberg Law, *http://www.bloomberglaw.com/public/desktop/document/Cone_v_Bell_1 29_S_Ct_1769_173_L_Ed_2d_701_2009_Court_Opinion?1459628723* Accessed Tuesday, March 22, 2016

26.
Bloomberg Law,
http://www.bloomberglaw.com/public/desktop/document/Cone_v_Bell_1
29_S_Ct_1769_173_L_Ed_2d_701_2009_Court_Opinion?1459628723
Accessed Tuesday, March 22, 2016

27.
Bloomberg Law,
http://www.bloomberglaw.com/public/desktop/document/Cone_v_Bell_1
29_S_Ct_1769_173_L_Ed_2d_701_2009_Court_Opinion?1459628723
Accessed Tuesday, March 22, 2016

28.
Bloomberg Law,
.http://www.bloomberglaw.com/public/desktop/document/Cone_v_Bell_1
29_S_Ct_1769_173_L_Ed_2d_701_2009_Court_Opinion?1459628723
Accessed Tuesday, March 22, 2016

29.
Bloomberg Law,
http://www.bloomberglaw.com/public/desktop/document/Cone_v_Bell_1
29_S_Ct_1769_173_L_Ed_2d_701_2009_Court_Opinion?1459628723
Accessed Tuesday, March 22, 2016

30.
Bloomberg Law,
http://www.bloomberglaw.com/public/desktop/document/Cone_v_Bell_1
29_S_Ct_1769_173_L_Ed_2d_701_2009_Court_Opinion?1459628723
Accessed Tuesday, March 22, 2016

31.
Bloomberg Law,
.http://www.bloomberglaw.com/public/desktop/document/Cone_v_Bell_1
29_S_Ct_1769_173_L_Ed_2d_701_2009_Court_Opinion?1459628723
Accessed Tuesday, March 22, 2016

32.
Bloomberg Law
http://www.bloomberglaw.com/public/desktop/document/Cone_v_Bell_1
29_S_Ct_1769_173_L_Ed_2d_701_2009_Court_Opinion?1459628723
Accessed Tuesday, March 22, 2016

33.
http://www.supremecourt.gov/oral_arguments/argument_transcripts/07-1114.pdf
Accessed Tuesday, March 22, 2016

34.
http://www.supremecourt.gov/oral_arguments/argument_transcripts/07-1114.pdf
Accessed Tuesday, March 22, 2016

35.
http://www.supremecourt.gov/oral_arguments/argument_transcripts/07-1114.pdf
Accessed Tuesday, March 22, 2016

36.
http://www.supremecourt.gov/oral_arguments/argument_transcripts/07-1114.pdf
Accessed Tuesday, March 22, 2016

37.
http://www.supremecourt.gov/oral_arguments/argument_transcripts/07-1114.pdf
Accessed Tuesday, March 22, 2016

38.
http://www.supremecourt.gov/oral_arguments/argument_transcripts/07-1114.pdf
Accessed Tuesday, March 22, 2016

39.
David Keenan, Deborah Jane Cooper, David Lebowitz & Tamar Lerer, The Myth of Prosecutorial Accountability After Connick v. Thompson: Why Existing Professional Responsibility Measures Cannot Protect Against Prosecutorial Misconduct, 121 Yale L.J. Online 203 (2011), http://yalelawjournal.org/forum/the-myth-of-prosecutorial-accountability-after-connick-v-thompson-why-existing-professional-responsibility-measures-cannot-protect-against-prosecutorial-misconduct
Accessed March 16, 2016

40.
American Bar Association
http://www.americanbar.org/groups/professional_responsibility/publicati
ons/model_rules_of_professional_conduct/rule_3_8_special_responsibili
ties_of_a_prosecutor.html
Accessed March 16, 2016

41.
David Keenan, Deborah Jane Cooper, David Lebowitz & Tamar Lerer,
The Myth of Prosecutorial Accountability After Connick v. Thompson:
Why Existing Professional Responsibility Measures Cannot Protect
Against Prosecutorial Misconduct, 121 Yale L.J. Online 203 (2011),
http://yalelawjournal.org/forum/the-myth-of-prosecutorial-
accountability-after-connick-v-thompson-why-existing-professional-
responsibility-measures-cannot-protect-against-prosecutorial-misconduct
Accessed March 16, 2016

42.
Ibid.

43.
Ibid.

44.
Ibid.

45.
American Bar Association
http://www.americanbar.org/publications/criminal_justice_section_archi
ve/crimjust_standards_pfunc_blk.html
Accessed April 1, 2016

46.
John Paul Stevens
http://www.supremecourt.gov/publicinfo/speeches/Equal%20Justice%20
Init%20Dinner%20(1606_001).pdf
Accessed Tuesday, March 22, 2016

47.
David Savage,http://articles.latimes.com/2010/jan/05/nation/la-na-court-framed5-2010jan05
Accessed March 26, 2016

48.
David Savage,http://articles.latimes.com/2010/jan/05/nation/la-na-court-framed5-2010jan05
Accessed March 26, 2016

49.
http://www.supremecourt.gov/oral_arguments/argument_transcripts/08-1065.pdf
Accessed March 26, 2016

50.
Ibid.

51.
Ibid.

52.
http://www.supremecourt.gov/publicinfo/speeches/Equal%20Justice%20Init%20Dinner%20(1606_001).pdf
Accessed Tuesday, March 22, 2016

53.
SCOTUS Blog
http://www.scotusblog.com/case-files/cases/connick-v-thompson/
Accessed April 7, 2016

54.
SCOTUS Blog
http://www.scotusblog.com/case-files/cases/smith-v-louisiana/
Accessed April 7, 2016

55.
Adam Liptak, http://www.nytimes.com/2011/11/09/us/supreme-court-rebukes-a-new-orleans-prosecutor.html?_r=0
Accessed March 26, 2016

56.
Bloomberg Law
http://www.bloomberglaw.com/public/desktop/document/Cone_v_Bell_
129_S_Ct_1769_173_L_Ed_2d_701_2009_Court_Opinion?1458955009
Accessed March 25, 2016

57.
Robert H. Jackson https://www.roberthjackson.org
24 J. Am. Jud. Soc'y 18 (1940), 31 J. Crim. L. 3 (1940) (address at
Conference of United States Attorneys, Washington, D.C., April 1,
1940).
Accessed March 26, 2016

58.
Henry Weinstein
http://articles.latimes.com/1993-11-04/local/me-53129_1_appeals-court-
prosecutors
Accessed March 29, 2016

59.
Ibid.

60.
Adam M. Gershowitz, "Prosecutorial Shaming: Naming Attorneys to
Reduce Prosecutorial Misconduct" (2009). *Faculty Publications.*
Paper 1254.
http://scholarship.law.wm.edu/cgi/viewcontent.cgi?article=2287&context
=facpubs
http://scholarship.law.wm.edu/facpubs/1254
Accessed April 6, 2016

61.
Alex Kozinski,http://georgetownlawjournal.org/articles/criminal-law-2-
0-preface-to-the-44th-annual-review-of-criminal-procedure/
Accessed March 29, 2016

62.
Ibid.

63.
Margaret Z. Johns, *Reconsidering Absolute Prosecutorial Immunity*, 2005 BYU L. Rev. 53 (2005)
http://digitalcommons.law.byu.edu/lawreview/vol2005/iss1/2
Accessed March 24, 2016

64.
Alexandra Natapoff
https://www.aclu.org/files/images/asset_upload_file744_30623.pdf
Accessed April 3, 2016

65.
Alexandra Natapoff, Snitching: The Institutional and Communal Consequences, Loyola Law School,
https://www.aclu.org/files/images/asset_upload_file744_30623.pdf
Accessed April 3, 2016

66.
Alexandra Natapoff, Snitching: The Institutional and Communal Consequences, Loyola Law School,
https://www.aclu.org/files/images/asset_upload_file744_30623.pdf
Accessed April 3, 2016

67.
Ryan Blitstein
http://www.alternet.org/story/144148/sex,_beer,_heroin_and_cocaine%3A_how_prosecutors_pay_off_criminal_snitches
Accessed March 26, 2016

68.
Cornell Law
https://www.law.cornell.edu/uscode/text/42/1983
Accessed April 6, 2016

69.
Margaret Z. Johns, *Reconsidering Absolute Prosecutorial Immunity*, 2005 BYU L. Rev. 53 (2005)
http://digitalcommons.law.byu.edu/lawreview/vol2005/iss1/2
Accessed March 24, 2016

70.
Ibid.

71.
Ibid.

72.
Cornell Law
https://www.law.cornell.edu/rules/frcp/rule_61
Accessed April 8, 2016

73.
James Edward Wicht III,*There is No Such Thing as a Harmless Constitutional Error: Returning to a Rule of Automatic Reversal*, 12 BYU J.
Pub. L. 73 (1997)
http://digitalcommons.law.byu.edu/jpl/vol12/iss1/3
Accessed April 8, 2016

74.
Ibid.

75.
Ibid.

76.
Brian Sun
http://www.sccla.org/resources/documents/articles/bsun_042011/article_bsun2.pdf
Accessed April 8, 2016

77.
David Keenan, Deborah Jane Cooper, David Lebowitz & Tamar Lerer, The Myth of Prosecutorial Accountability After Connick v. Thompson: Why Existing Professional Responsibility Measures Cannot Protect Against Prosecutorial Misconduct, 121 Yale L.J. Online 203 (2011), http://yalelawjournal.org/forum/the-myth-of-prosecutorial-accountability-after-connick-v-thompson-why-existing-professional-responsibility-measures-cannot-protect-against-prosecutorial-misconduct.
Accessed March 24, 2016

78.
Keenan, David; Cooper, Deborah Jane; Lebowitz, David; and Lerer, Tamar, "The Myth of Prosecutorial Accountability After Connick v. Thompson: Why Existing Professional Responsibility Measures Cannot Protect Against Prosecutorial Misconduct" (2012). *Student Prize Papers*. Paper 103.
http://digitalcommons.law.yale.edu/ylsspps_papers/103
Accessed March 24, 2016

79.
Alex Kozinski
https://www.princeton.edu/~ereading/USvOlsen.pdf
Accessed April 8, 2016

80.
Techdirt
https://www.techdirt.com/articles/20150715/11374931651/judge-kozinski-theres-very-little-justice-our-so-called-justice-system.shtml
Accessed March 30, 2016

81.
https://supreme.justia.com/cases/federal/us/509/259/
Accessed April 9, 2016

82.
Cornell Law
https://www.law.cornell.edu/supct/html/91-7849.ZO.html
Accessed April 9, 2016

83.
Cornell Law
https://www.law.cornell.edu/supct/html/91-7849.ZO.html
Accessed April 9, 2016

84.
https://supreme.justia.com/cases/federal/us/509/259/
Accessed April 9, 2016

85.
Cornell Law
https://www.law.cornell.edu/supct/html/91-7849.ZO.html
Accessed April 9, 2016

86.
Margaret Z. Johns, *Reconsidering Absolute Prosecutorial Immunity*,
2005 BYU L. Rev. 53 (2005) P 67
http://digitalcommons.law.byu.edu/lawreview/vol2005/iss1/2
Accessed March 24, 2016

87
Ibid.

88.
Ibid.

89.
Bennett L. Gershman, The Prosecutor's Duty to Truth, 14 Geo. J. Legal
Ethics 309 (2001) http://digitalcommons.pace.edu/lawfaculty/128/
Accessed March 24, 2016

90.
Ivan E. Bodensteiner, *Congress Needs to Repair the Court's Damage to
§ 1983*, 16 Tex. J. C.L. & C.R. 29 (2010).

91.
Henry Weinstein, http://www.law.uci.edu/faculty/full-time/weinstein/
Accessed March 29, 2016

92.
Henry Weinstein
http://articles.latimes.com/1993-10-04/local/me-42104 1 court-judges
Accessed March 29, 2016
93.
Ibid.

94.
Ibid.

95.

Henry Weinstein, http//articles.latimes.com/1993-11-04/local/me-53129
1 appeals-court-prosecutors
Accessed March 29, 2016

96.

Alexandra Natapoff, Snitching: The Institutional and Communal
Consequences, Loyola Law School,
https://www.aclu.org/files/images/asset_upload_file744_30623.pdf
Accessed April 3, 2016

97.

Eugene Volokh
www.washingtonpost.com/news/volokh-conspiracy/wp/2015/07/14/12-
reasons-to-worry-about-our-criminal-justice-system-from-a-prominent-
conservative-federal-judge/
Accessed March 22, 2106

98.

National Registry of Exonerations
http://www.law.umich.edu/special/exoneration/Pages/Exonerations-in-
the-United-States-Map.aspx
Accessed April 13, 2016

99.

Margaret Z. Johns, *Reconsidering Absolute Prosecutorial Immunity*,
2005 BYU L. Rev. 53 (2005)
http://digitalcommons.law.byu.edu/lawreview/vol2005/iss1/2
Accessed March 24, 2016

100.

John Paul Stevens, http://caselaw.findlaw.com/us-supreme-
court/471/808.html
Accessed March 22, 2016

101.

http://www1.law.umkc.edu/justicepapers/TuttleDocs/TuttleMainPage.ht
ml
Accessed March 22, 2016

102.
http://georgetownlawjournal.org/articles/criminal-law-2-0-preface-to-
the-44th-annual-review-of-criminal-procedure/
Accessed March 29, 2016

103.
Robert H. Jackson,
https://www.justice.gov/sites/default/files/ag/legacy/2011/09/16/04-01-
1940.pdf
Accessed March 26, 2016

104.
Alexandra Natapoff, Snitching: The Institutional and Communal
Consequences, Loyola Law School,
https://www.aclu.org/files/images/asset_upload_file744_30623.pdf
Accessed April 3, 2016

105.
Alexandra Natapoff, Snitching: The Institutional and Communal
Consequences, Loyola Law School,
https://www.aclu.org/files/images/asset_upload_file744_30623.pdf
Accessed April 3, 2016

BIBLIOGRAPHY

American Bar Association. *Rule 3.8: Special Responsibilities of a Prosecutor.* Assessed March 16, 2106.
http://www.americanbar.org/groups/professional_responsibility/publications/model_rules_of_professional_conduct/rule_3_8_special_responsibilities_of_a_prosecutor.html

American Bar Association. *Prosecution Function.* Assessed April 1, 2016.
http://www.americanbar.org/publications/criminal_justice_section_archive/crimjust_standards_pfunc_blk.html

Blitstein, Ryan. *Sex, Beer, Heroin and Cocaine. How Prosecutors Pay Off Criminal Snitches.* Accessed March 26, 2016
http://www.alternet.org/story/144148/sex,_beer,_heroin_and_cocaine%3A_how_prosecutors_pay_off_criminal_snitches.

Bloomberg Law. *Cone v Bell.* Cone v Bell. Assessed March 22. 2016.
http://www.bloomberglaw.com/public/desktop/document/Cone_v_Bell_1 29_S_Ct_1769_173_L_Ed_2d_701_2009_Court_Opinion?1459628723

Bloomberg Law. *Cone v Bell.* Assessed March 25, 2106
http://www.bloomberglaw.com/public/desktop/document/Cone_v_Bell_129_S_Ct_1769_173_L_Ed_2d_701_2009_Court_Opinion?1458955009

Bodensteiner, Ivan E.. *Congress Needs to Repair the Court's Damage to § 1983.* 16 Tex. J. C.L. & C.R. 29 (2010).

Cornell Law. *Buckley V Fitzsimmons (91-7849).* Assessed April 9, 2016.
https://www.law.cornell.edu/supct/html/91-7849.ZO.html

Cornell Law. *42 US Code Section 1983- Civil Action for Deprivation of Rights.* Assessed April 6, 2016.
https://www.law.cornell.edu/uscode/text/42/1983

Cornell Law. *Rule 61. Harmless Error.* Accessed April 8, 2016.
https://www.law.cornell.edu/rules/frcp/rule_61

Gershman, Bennett L. *The Prosecutor's Duty to Truth, 14 Geo. J. Legal Ethics 309 (2001)* Accessed March 24, 2016
http://digitalcommons.pace.edu/lawfaculty/128/.

Gershowitz, Adam M., *"Prosecutorial Shaming: Naming Attorneys to Reduce Prosecutorial Misconduct"* (2009). *Faculty Publications.* Paper 1254. Assessed April 6, 2016. http://scholarship.law.wm.edu/facpubs/1254

Jackson, Robert H.. *The Federal Prosecutor.* Accessed March 26, 2016. https://www.justice.gov/sites/default/files/ag/legacy/2011/09/16/04-01-1940.pdf

Jackson, Robert H. *Robert H. Jackson Biography.* Accessed March 16, 2016. https://www.roberthjackson.org/article/robert-h-jackson-biography/

Johns, Margaret Z. *Reconsidering Absolute Prosecutorial Immunity,* 2005 BYU L. Rev. 53 (2005). Assessed March 24, 2016.

http://digitalcommons.law.byu.edu/lawreview/vol2005/iss1/2 Accessed March 24, 2016

Justia. *Buckley v. Fitzsimmons 509 U.S. 259 (1993).* Assessed April 9, 2016 https://supreme.justia.com/cases/federal/us/509/259/

Keenan, David. Cooper, Deborah Jane. Lebowitz, David. Lerer, Tamar. The Myth of Prosecutorial Accountability After Connick v. Thompson: Why Existing Professional Responsibility Measures Cannot Protect Against Prosecutorial Misconduct. Assessed March 28, 2016. http://yalelawjournal.org/forum/the-myth-of-prosecutorial-accountability-after-connick-v-thompson-why-existing-professional-responsibility-measures-cannot-protect-against-prosecutorial-misconduct

Kozinski, Alex. *Criminal Law 2.0.* Assessed March 29, 2016. http://georgetownlawjournal.org/articles/criminal-law-2-0-preface-to-the-44th-annual-review-of-criminal-procedure/

Kozinski, Alex. *Dissent by Chief Judge Kozinski, United States of America v. Kenneth R. Olsen.* Assessed April 8, 2016. https://www.princeton.edu/~ereading/USvOlsen.pdf

Liptak, Adam. *Supreme Court Rebukes a New Orleans Prosecutor.* Assessed March 26, 2016. http://www.nytimes.com/2011/11/09/us/supreme-court-rebukes-a-new-orleans-prosecutor.html?_r=0

Natapoff, Alexandra. *Snitching: The Institutional and Communal Consequences*. Assessed April 3, 2016.
https://www.aclu.org/files/images/asset_upload_file744_30623.pdf

National Registry of Exonerations. *Exonerations in the United States.* Assessed April 13, 2016.
http://www.law.umich.edu/special/exoneration/Pages/Exonerations-in-the-United-States-Map.aspx

Officer Down Memorial Page. *United States Department of the Treasury - Internal Revenue Service - Criminal Investigation, Line of Duty Deaths.* Assessed April 14, 2016
https://www.odmp.org/agency/3962-united-states-department-of-the-treasury-internal-revenue-service-criminal-investigation-us-government

Russell, Jason, *Look at How Many Pages are in the Federal Tax Code.Washington Examiner.* Assessed April 14, 2106
http://www.washingtonexaminer.com/look-at-how-many-pages-are-in-the-federal-tax-code/article/2563032

SCOTUSblog. *Connick v Thompson.* Assessed April 7, 2016.
http://www.scotusblog.com/case-files/cases/connick-v-thompson/

SCOTUSblog. *Smith v Louisiana.* Assessed April 7, 2016.
http://www.scotusblog.com/case-files/cases/smith-v-louisiana/

Savage, David. *Prosecutor Conduct case before Supreme Court is Settled.* Assessed. March 26, 2016.
http://articles.latimes.com/2010/jan/05/nation/la-na-court-framed5-2010jan05

Stevens, John Paul. *Find Law, Oklahoma City v Tuttle.* Assessed March 22, 2106.
http://caselaw.findlaw.com/us-supreme-court/471/808.html

Stevens, John Paul. *Equal Justice Initiative Dinner Honoring Justice Stevens.* Assessed March 22, 2016
http://www.supremecourt.gov/publicinfo/speeches/Equal%20Justice%20Init%20Dinner%20(1606_001).pdf

Sun, Brian A. *The Overzealous Prosecutor.* Assessed April 8, 2016
http://www.sccla.org/resources/documents/articles/bsun_042011/article_bsun2.pdf

Supreme Court of the United States. *Gary Bradford Cone v Ricky Bell, Warden.* Assessed March 22, 2106.
http://www.supremecourt.gov/oral_arguments/argument_transcripts/07-1114.pdf

Supreme Court of the United States. *Pottawattamie County, Iowa, et al., v. Curtis W. McGhee, Jr., et al.* Assessed March 26, 2016
http://www.supremecourt.gov/oral_arguments/argument_transcripts/08-1065.pdf

Techdirt. Assessed March 30, 2016.
https://www.techdirt.com/articles/20150715/11374931651/judge-kozinski-theres-very-little-justice-our-so-called-justice-system.shtml

UMKC School of Law. *Oklahoma City v Tuttle. 471 U.S. 808 (1985).* Assessed March 22, 2016
http://www1.law.umkc.edu/justicepapers/TuttleDocs/TuttleMainPage.htm

Volokh, Eugene. *Twelve Reasons to Worry About Our Criminal Justice System from a Prominent Conservative Federal Judge.* Assessed March 22, 2106
www.washingtonpost.com/news/volokh-conspiracy/wp/2015/07/14/12-reasons-to-worry-about-our-criminal-justice-system-from-a-prominent-conservative-federal-judge/

Weinstein, Henry. *Court Will Not Name Reprimanded Prosecutor.* LA Times. Accessed March 29, 2016.
http://articles.latimes.com/1993-11-04/local/me-53129_1_appeals-court-prosecutors

Weinstein, Henry. *U.S. Attorney Asks Court to Erase Criticism.* Assessed March 29, 2016.
http://articles.latimes.com/1993-10-04/local/me-42104_1_court-judges

University of California, Irvine School of Law. *Henry Weinstein.* Assessed March 29, 2016.
http://www.law.uci.edu/faculty/full-time/weinstein/

Wechler, Robert. *The Special Responsibilities of Prosecutors- and Other Local Government Attorneys.* Assessed. April 1, 2016.
http://www.cityethics.org/node/460

Wicht, James Edward, III. *There is No Such Thing as a Harmless Constitutional Error: Returning to a Rule of Automatic Reversal,* 12 BYU J.Pub. L. 73 (1997) Assessed March 29, 2016 http://digitalcommons.law.byu.edu/jpl/vol12/iss1/3

www.ingramcontent.com/pod-product-compliance
Lightning Source LLC
Chambersburg PA
CBHW060027030426
42334CB00019B/2205